THE LOST

The

Lost Lunar

Baedeker

POEMS OF

Mina Loy

EDITED BY ROGER L. CONOVER

CARCANET

FRONTISPIECE
Mina Loy, 1909. Stephen Haweis photograph.

First published by Farrar, Straus & Giroux, Inc., New York.

First published in Great Britain in 1997 by
Carcanet Press Limited
4th Floor, Conavon Court
12–16 Blackfriars Street
Manchester M3 5BQ

A CIP record for this book
is available from the British Library.
ISBN 1 85754 326 2

The publisher acknowledges financial assistance
from the Arts Council of England.

Printed and bound by Antony Rowe Ltd, Eastbourne

This book is Mina Loy's to give

to Arthur Cravan, Joella Bayer, and Fabienne Benedict.

With their blessing, it is also for Case, Strand, and Anna

CONTENTS

IV COMPENSATIONS OF POVERTY
(POEMS 1942-1949)

V EXCAVATIONS & PRECISIONS
(PROSE 1914–1925)

APPENDICES

Introduction

For a brief period early in the twentieth century, Mina Loy was the Belle of the American Poetry Ball. But by the end of the century, most had forgotten she was there at all.

On the evening of May 25, 1917, Mina Loy and Marcel Duchamp made their way to Greenwich Village's "ultra bohemian, prehistoric, post-alcoholic" Webster Hall, where the twenty-third and final "Pagan Romp" of the season was just getting under way. The run-down community center on East Eleventh Street was known as "the Devil's Playhouse" by bourgeoisie and bohemians alike. It had earned that moniker not just from the antics of locals but from the stunts that expatriates performed at the freewheeling frolics. To them, Webster Hall was reminiscent of Left Bank reunions before the war. It was a place where exiles and Villagers could mingle as one tribe, and where outlandish behavior was not only tolerated but applauded. The costumes required for admission made it possible for anyone who wished to revel out of character or gender to do so undercover.

On this particular night, Marcel Duchamp (a.k.a. Rrose Sélavy) was male in habit and Mina Loy was dressed in a costume of her own design. They were the model expatriate couple, in disguise. A little magazine that Duchamp edited and Loy wrote for was celebrating the publication of its second number. Dadaist in spirit, *The Blind Man* advertised "continuous syncopation" until dawn. The advertisement on the inside front cover threatened to banish to box seats anyone who arrived in conventional clothing. When the ball was over, Duchamp and four companions—Mina Loy among them—breakfasted on scrambled eggs and wine, before stumbling into Duchamp's bed, where the *ménage à cinq* spent a chaste night.

Such scenes are typical of how—until Carolyn Burke's biography recovered her extraordinary life—Mina Loy has been recalled. As part of a group. As slightly out of focus. As someone's mistress. As a guest at a ball. Loy's name is most often found in a string of names, as the emblematic avant-gardist, the bohemian's bohemian, the nervy "impuritan" making the rounds of Village cafés and European salons. She makes colorful appearances in dozens of biographies: in those of Djuna Barnes, Constantin Brancusi, Ernest Hemingway, James Joyce, Wyndham Lewis, Marianne Moore, Ezra Pound, Gertrude Stein, Wallace Stevens, Alfred Stieglitz, and William Carlos Williams, for example. In memoir after modernist memoir, she has been granted a forceful personality, a cerebral bearing, a perfect complexion, and a sexual body. But not a voice.

First and last, this book is an attempt to restore a great poet's lost voice. I use "great" advisedly, mindful that Loy has never been called great before. But mindful, too, that "great" modern writers—among them Basil Bunting, Eliot, Pound, Stein, and Williams—praised her work. Some even conceded their debt to her.

Given Loy's reclusiveness in her later years, the fact that she published only two books during her lifetime, and her seeming lack of concern—in interviews and conversations, at least—with building a reputation, or an *oeuvre*, it is not surprising that her few rediscoverers have pressed her case with an assiduousness reserved for the most self-effacing of poets. "I was never a poet," she once proclaimed. But she had her own idea of how to package beauty and talent, and in letters to friends she often seemed hungry for recognition, even as she courted obscurity: "Can't you write about me as a hidden wrinkle—the only woman who has been decided enough to forego easy success—etc etc—uninterrupted by the potency of beauty . . . ?" she appealed to Carl Van Vechten in 1915. There was a rumor circulating around Paris in the twenties that Mina Loy was in fact not a real person at all but a made-up persona. Upon hearing this, the story goes, Loy turned up at Natalie Barney's salon in order to make her presence known: "I assure you that I am indeed a live being. But it is necessary to stay very unknown . . . To maintain my incognito, the hazard I chose was—poet." Upon finishing her novel, *Insel*, she professed she hadn't a clue as to its merit, then offhanded a remark suggesting both perfect indifference and confidence verging on premonition as to its literary fate: "I leave that to my post-mortem examination." The novel languished unread for decades. Finally, in 1991, it was published. As we continue the posthumous examination she predicted, do we take her at her word, and if so, which word?

If her statements are self-erasing, they are also Duchampian. They belie their nonchalance, as did his. Throughout her career, Loy camouflaged demonstrative and theatrical first persons behind inscrutable aliases. She ventriloquized. She dissembled. She canceled. Whether this was part of a conscious design to elude critical framing or an involuntary strategy for survival is difficult to say; indeed, there may be no distinction. She assumes both self-deprecatory and defiant voices in her poems, sometimes delivering cruelty with such precision that it seems a form of compassion. Figuratively, then, the rumor in Paris was true: she made herself up. She appeared when she was least expected. She was disruptive. This book is presented in that spirit. Twentieth-century poetry's lost guidebook surfaces after we thought all the evidence was in.

Mina Loy's goal was quite simply to become the most original woman of her generation. To this end, but sometimes to our confusion, she refused identification with many groups and causes that seemed natural for her to adopt. She affiliated herself, instead, with those considered the "enemy" by the more "ideologically correct" of her generation. Rather than allowing herself to be fixed by an identity, she interloped, using her various identities to transform the cultures and social milieus she inhabited. Feminist and Futurist, wife and lover, militant and pacifist, actress and model, Christian Scientist and nurse, she was the binarian's nightmare. She was a Futurist, Dadaist, Surrealist, feminist, conceptualist, modernist, post-modernist, and none of the above. Her anti-career, if you like, was marked by so many seeming contradictions, counter-allegiances, and inconsistencies that she was often considered unbalanced. She scripted her own political platforms and composed didactic manifestos. She wrote pseudo-scientific theories of facial destiny and composed one of the most radical polemics ever written on feminism. She wore femininity as a mask, sometimes to disguise what she often called her "masculine side," sometimes to draw the masculine to her side and sometimes to make her feminism less threatening. Loy wore mask upon mask; she was a poet of sophistication, in the word's true sense. She knew something about constructing myth, and she knew something about violating the rules of heterosexual discourse. Like Duchamp, she was a confusing package for America, the land without myth and the land of gender.

Loy came to the United States in 1916 by way of England, Paris, and Florence, but her reputation preceded her. No sooner had she arrived than she was being profiled as the avatar of the New Woman and the last word in modern verse. Like Duchamp's, Loy's artistic and intellectual *habillement* was perceived as impeccably avant-garde and international. Pound saw Marianne Moore and Loy as equals, but when Moore found herself in Loy's company, she was decidedly uncomfortable. Amy Lowell was so incensed by Alfred Kreymborg's publication of Loy's poetic treatise on sexual discontent ("Love Songs") that she refused to submit any more work to *Others* magazine. Loy was considered the most dangerous of the radical "Otherists." If she didn't like what critics said about her, she shamed them with wit, turning their words against them. Many of her early poems are satirical portraits of her former lovers, or songs of disillusion about sex, childbirth, or romance. She was as likely to turn upon those who praised her as on those who took exception. At times she seemed as bent on excommunication as at other times she was eager for communication. She ridiculed Pound and Eliot, even after they commented favorably on her verse. She genuflected to no one.

It was probably based on such impressions that Moore wrote "Those Various Scalpels," a poem which Patricia Willis has suggested (rightly, in my view) is a portrait of Loy. Moore questions the ruthless purpose which Loy's talents served: "Are they weapons or scalpels?" Like virtually every contemporary who wrote about Loy, Moore takes measure of Loy's intelligence, beauty, and diction, then calls these qualities into question, turning observations into accusations. How could one so beautiful, Harriet Monroe wondered—and Monroe considered Loy that, if nothing else ("beauty ever-young which has survived four babies," she said of Loy after their first encounter)—how could one so beautiful be so unsparing in her revelation of the ugliness in herself, and so sardonic about love?

Many of Loy's early critics objected to the use of intellectual formulations and archaic vocabulary in her verse. They found her diction artificial, decorative. They did not understand that she was building a Trojan verse—deliberately hijacking Victorian vocabulary and conceptual posturing in order to subvert the values and expose the mechanisms such constructions were meant to euphemize. Her poetry divided even the *Others* group, which usually closed ranks around its own. In a 1919 review of *Others*, Conrad Aiken encouraged readers to "pass lightly over the . . . tentacular quiverings of Mina Loy" in favor of the "manly metres" of Eliot and Stevens. John Collier's review was also typical. He cited Loy's verse as an example of "the need for objective standards related to . . . tradition," and accused her of producing work "in which the terminology is so stilted, so consciously artificial," and so full of "quasi-scientific pomposities" that only by "some monstrous exertion of faith, or self-hypnotism [could] its accumulator . . . regard the results of her labour as poetry."

Yet Ezra Pound, in 1921, thought Loy, Moore, and Williams were the only poets in America writing anything of interest in verse. Five years later, Yvor Winters invoked Emily Dickinson as Loy's only forerunner. Like Dickinson, Loy was writing at a time when readers still noticed the absence of pleasures denied them. Loy withheld traditional meter, rhyme, and syntax, and presented sex with the expediency of an invoice. She broke every rule on the page, made up her own grammar, invented her own words—even improvised her own punctuation. She drew her vocabulary from one of the most curio-filled lexical cabinets in twentieth-century poetry, yet she remained unseduced by the melodies of conversation and unreceptive to the conventions of versification. Her readers, like Dickinson's, were wary of the sound of an alien voice. It was Loy's "otherness" that was noticed first and foremost by her contemporaries. "Her poems would have puzzled Grandma," ran the caption beneath her photograph in the *New York Evening Sun* four months after she arrived in New York, accompanying a profile that depicted her as that rare and exotic species, *la nouvelle femme.* "No natural history contains her habitat . . . If she isn't the modern woman, who is, pray?" the *Sun* reporter understated. Dickinson was received as poetry's queer aunt when her poems first appeared one hundred years ago; Loy was perceived as poetry's deviant daughter following the appearance of "Love Songs" twenty years later. Fin-de-siècle criticism nearly put Dickinson's work into the closet for a quarter-century. In Loy's case, the door shut sooner and faster.

The first doors to open to Loy were in America, and did so before she arrived. But they closed soon after she got here. Critics who knew her felt that her demeanor was out of line with her verse. Carl Van Vechten, the photographer and music critic, was also her first informal agent. He considered Loy the most beautiful of a beautiful generation of poets. She had great promise as a poet, he thought, if only she would stop writing about sex. Her first husband, Stephen Haweis, warned his wife along similar lines: *Keep writing that way, Mina Haweis, and you'll lose your good name.* Alfred Kreymborg, one of her first editors, summarized the public's prevailing objections: if she could dress like a lady, why couldn't she write like one? But there were other problems as well. When Loy came to America, she made it known that she was here to use her talents. She wrote plays and stories as well as poetry. Not only that: she acted, painted, made lampshades, sculpted, modeled, designed dresses, and patented inventions. This was unacceptable. In a provincial land, it was all right for a woman to express herself as a solitary genius, or to be a beauty, but not to be a beautiful intellectual and a creative person-at-large. Villagers respected artistic exclusiveness. Loy respected no such bounds and addressed her sarcastic "Apology of Genius" to those who

> *turn on us your smooth fools' faces*
> *like buttocks bared in aboriginal mockeries . . .*

What she named an apology was no apology at all. She claimed that geniuses were exempt from judgment:

> *Our wills are formed*
> *by curious disciplines*
> *beyond your laws . . .*

Shortly after her arrival in the States, Loy gave her first public reading. William Rose Benét, Maxwell Bodenheim, Padraic Colum, and William Carlos Williams joined her on the mezzanine of Grand Central Palace on Independents Poets Day. Some came out of curiosity, not only to listen but to ogle. Who was this Mina Loy? Was she the great beauty the gossips described? Were her poems as strange as they were reputed to be by people who were passing around copies of magazines with odd names like *Trend, Rogue,* and *The Blind Man* before her reading?

When Pound first introduced American readers to Mina Loy, he described her verse as authentically American. "These girls," he said of Loy and Moore, wrote "something which would not have come out of any other country." Pound was being disingenuous about Loy's origins. Surely he knew that she was English. But he had a point. Loy never belonged to England, and her work was never published there. But what Pound couldn't know was that America, the country Loy adopted, would never adopt her.

Eighty years later, an editor again finds himself introducing Loy to American readers for the first time, and finds many of the same questions still being asked. Metrically, what effect was she seeking, if any? How knowingly was she mocking the lyric tradition? How deliberately was she distorting diction? Was she consciously skating a fine line of prosodic disaster, only to rescue herself time after time, like a naturally balletic dancer with inebriate tendencies, in order to make us realize that awkwardness itself can be a desired effect, because its solution—recovery—delivers more tension and relief, and commands more attention than grace executed predictably?

Today, some new questions are being asked. Exactly which poets did she read with profit? What is it that makes her unassimilable by the canonists? Did she know how precociously her language assailed the fortresses of gender? How do we distinguish a posture of seduction from a gesture of authority? Did she lead the avant-garde in adopting a guise of transgressive femininity as a masquerade? And the big questions, I suppose: Was she ever really at home in English? Was she an American poet? And how much control did she have over the publication of *Lunar Baedeker*? Some of these questions are addressed in the Notes, which present information on the way her work was originally published and perceived. Other questions are addressed by Loy herself in a newly discovered text "On Modern Poetry."

The publication of this book at four minutes to the millennium, so to speak, means that Loy has a chance to rise above neglect. But in order to read her, we not only have to get past neglect; we have to get past legend. And this may prove more difficult, for legend has a way of insinuating itself upon neglect. I first edited Loy's work in 1982. At the time, publishing her work felt more like a cause than an editorial occasion. *The Last Lunar Baedeker* circulated like a secret handshake, and has since become part of the Loy myth. That myth takes its shape from many sources, some of Loy's own making: the diaries of a rebellious young woman, raised in a Victorian English household, who defected to French bohemian intellectual life and Italian Futurism; the memories of contemporaries who described an opinionated, intransigent, witty seductress who left two children with a nurse in Florence to come to New York, and who returned, two years later, pregnant by a missing husband, only to leave again; the deaths of two children; the images of her passionate affair with a poet-boxer who later became a patron saint of the Dadaists, and her search for him in Mexican morgues and prisons; the stories of a lonely widow practicing Christian Science and holding séances in a Bowery rooming house; the exhibition organized by her old friend Marcel Duchamp in 1959, featuring beatific visions of bums fashioned from trash. These stories should neither elevate nor diminish Loy's stature as a poet. She should first be apprehended at poem-level.

Mina Loy is not for everyone. It is not by accident that her work has been misplaced. "Difficult" is the word that has been most often used to describe her. Difficult as a poet and difficult as a person. And certainly difficult to place. Her work has never attracted casual readers. It is easiest simply to ignore her. Until now, the determination required to *find* her poems, let alone the perspicacity required to *read* them, has served as a qualifying experience. But her readers, if small in number, have also been large in commitment. Once discovered, if her poems do not immediately repel, they possess. Her work is far more likely to be a toxic or a tonic—quickly sworn off or gradually acquired as a lifelong habit—than a passing interest. In my own experience, and that of many people with whom I have shared her work over the past twenty years, her poems either embed themselves deeply within the imagination or they alienate. With Loy, there is no in between. She is not an academic poet, but her poems are of the intellect. In order to read her with profit, you need at least four things: patience, intelligence, experience, and a dictionary.

One generally takes Loy—or does not—as one takes a vow. She tends to be accepted or avoided. No one considers her "decent." She is contrary, she is antimetric, and certainly she is *in*decent. Her first readers found her so, and most contemporary readers still do. You become either a sworn believer or a fast enemy. Loy's poetry has gradually fostered community among scholars, but it has also helped to define the sides of a poetry war which is quite real. In recent years her poetry has begun to register with a critical valence for the first time since the 1920s; this is new. But there will always remain those who don't subscribe. She forces us to take sides, and the easiest side to take is the one that looks past her. That is all right, for I believe, finally, that she will establish the reputations of critics more than they will hers, and that a true and good argument about Mina Loy has begun. That argument is needed. There is no version of the twentieth-century canon that includes Mina Loy's work, yet somehow it has survived. Perhaps her absence from such lists is itself a form of status. Perhaps it was her wish to remain unchosen.

It is not given to each of us
To be desired.

Loy once said in *The Blind Man:* "Art is *The Divine Joke,* and any Public . . . can see a nice easy simple joke such as the sun." She named her lunar baedeker not for the sun but for its ghost. It is now, just as the sun is setting on the century, that her guide to the moon seems indispensable. How strange her voice still seems. And how disturbing.

I believe there are certain guidebooks we should take with us as we navigate our way toward the next century, and that Mina Loy's is one of them. I think her poems have a relevance to the formation of a new modernity, and that she might yet prove to be the poet of her century, as Duchamp proved to be the artist of his. For some of us, she is already.

R.L.C.

I

FUTURISM × FEMINISM:

THE CIRCLE SQUARED

(POEMS 1914–1920)

*Loy in Florence, ca. 1909, holding her daughter, Joella,
and wearing a hat and dress of her own design*

There is no Life or Death,
Only activity
And in the absolute
Is no declivity.
There is no Love or Lust
Only propensity
Who would possess
Is a nonentity.
There is no First or Last
Only equality
And who would rule
Joins the majority.
There is no Space or Time
Only intensity,
And tame things
Have no immensity.

Parturition

I am the centre
Of a circle of pain
Exceeding its boundaries in every direction

The business of the bland sun
Has no affair with me
In my congested cosmos of agony
From which there is no escape
On infinitely prolonged nerve-vibrations
Or in contraction
To the pin-point nucleus of being

Locate an irritation   without
It is   within
                                         Within
It is without
The sensitized area
Is identical   with the extensity
Of intension

I am the false quantity
In the harmony of physiological potentiality
To which
Gaining self-control
I should be consonant
In time

Pain is no stronger than the resisting force
Pain calls up in me
The struggle is equal

The open window is full of a voice
A fashionable portrait-painter
Running up-stairs to a woman's apartment
Sings

> "All the girls are tid'ly did'ly
> All the girls are nice
> Whether they wear their hair in curls
> Or—"

At the back of the thoughts to which I permit crystallization
The conception   Brute
Why?
      The irresponsibility of the male
Leaves woman her superior Inferiority
He is running up-stairs

I am climbing a distorted mountain of agony
Incidentally with the exhaustion of control
I reach the summit
And gradually subside into anticipation of
Repose
Which never comes
For another mountain is growing up
Which   goaded by the unavoidable
I must traverse
Traversing myself

Something in the delirium of night-hours
Confuses while intensifying sensibility
Blurring spatial contours
So aiding elusion of the circumscribed
That the gurgling of a crucified wild beast
Comes from so far away
And the foam on the stretched muscles of a mouth
Is no part of myself
There is a climax in sensibility
When pain surpassing itself
Becomes Exotic

And the ego succeeds in unifying the positive and negative
   poles of sensation
Uniting the opposing and resisting forces
In lascivious revelation

Relaxation
Negation of myself as a unit
         Vacuum interlude
I should have been emptied of life
Giving life
For consciousness in crises   races
Through the subliminal deposits of evolutionary processes
Have I not
Somewhere
Scrutinized
A dead white feathered moth
Laying eggs?
A moment
Being realization
Can
Vitalized by cosmic initiation
Furnish an adequate apology
For the objective
Agglomeration of activities
Of a life.
LIFE
A leap with nature
Into the essence
Of unpredicted Maternity
Against my thigh
Touch of infinitesimal motion
Scarcely perceptible
Undulation
Warmth   moisture
Stir of incipient life
Precipitating into me
The contents of the universe

Mother I am
Identical
With infinite Maternity
   Indivisible
   Acutely
   I am absorbed
   Into
The was—is—ever—shall—be
Of cosmic reproductivity

Rises from the subconscious
Impression of a cat
With blind kittens
Among her legs
Same undulating life-stir
I am that cat

Rises from the sub-conscious
Impression of small animal carcass
Covered with blue-bottles
—Epicurean—
And through the insects
Waves that same undulation of living
Death
Life
I am knowing
All about
   Unfolding

The next morning
Each woman-of-the-people
Tip-toeing the red pile of the carpet
Doing hushed service
Each woman-of-the-people
Wearing a halo
A ludicrous little halo
Of which she is sublimely   unaware

I once heard in a church
—Man and woman God made them—
Thank God.

Italian Pictures

July in Vallombrosa

Old lady sitting still
Pine trees standing quite still
Sisters of mercy   whispering
Oust the Dryad

O consecration of forest
To the uneventful

I cannot imagine anything
Less disputably respectable
Than prolonged invalidism in Italy
At the beck
Of a British practitioner

Of all permissible pastimes
Attendant upon chastity
The one with which you can most efficiently insult
Life
Is your hobby of collecting death-beds
Blue Nun

So wrap the body in flannel and wool
Of superior quality from the Anglo-American
Until that ineffable moment
When Rigor Mortis
Divests it of its innate impurity

While round the hotel
Wanton Italian matrons
Discuss the better business of bed-linen
To regular puncture of needles

The old lady has a daughter
Who has been spent
In chasing moments from one room to another
When the essence of an hour
Was in its passing
With the passionate breath
Of the bronchitis-kettle
And her last little lust
Lost itself in a saucer of gruel

But all this moribund stuff
Is not wasted
For there is always Nature
So its expensive upkeep
Goes to support
The loves
Of head-waiters

The Costa San Giorgio

We English make a tepid blot
On the messiness
Of the passionate Italian life-traffic
Throbbing the street   up   steep
Up   up   to the porta
Culminating
In the stained frescoe of the dragon-slayer

The hips of women sway
Among the crawling children they produce
And the church hits the barracks
Where
The greyness of marching men
Falls through the greyness of stone

Oranges half-rotten are sold at a reduction
Hoarsely advertised as broken heads
BROKEN HEADS   and the barber
Has an imitation mirror
And Mary preserve our mistresses from seeing us as we see
   ourselves
Shaving
ICE CREAM
Licking is larger than mouths
Boots than feet
Slip   Slap   and the string dragging
And the angle of the sun
Cuts the whole lot in half

And warms the folded hands
Of a consumptive
Left outside   her chair is broken
And she wonders how we feel
For we walk very quickly
The noonday cannon
Having scattered the neighbour's pigeons

The smell of small cooking
From luckier houses
Is cruel to the maimed cat
Hiding
Among the carpenter's shavings
From three boys
—One holding a bar—
Who nevertheless
Born of human parents
Cry when locked in the dark

Fluidic blots of sky
Shift among roofs
Between bandy legs
Jerk patches of street

Interrupted by clacking
Of all the green shutters
From which
Bits of bodies
Variously leaning
Mingle eyes with the commotion

For there is little to do
The false pillow-spreads
Hugely initialed
Already adjusted
On matrimonial beds
And the glint on the china virgin
Consummately dusted

Having been thrown
Anything or something
That might have contaminated intimacy
OUT
Onto the middle of the street

Costa Magic

                    Her father
Indisposed to her marriage
And a rabid man at that
My most sympathetic daughter
Make yourself a conception
As large as this one
Here
But with yellow hair

From the house
Issuing   Sunday dressed
Combed precisely
                    SPLOSH

Pours something
Viscuous
Malefic
Unfamiliar

While listening up   I hear my husband
Mumbling   Mumbling
Mumbling   at the window
    Malediction
    Incantation
Under an hour
Her hand to her side   pressing
    Suffering
Being bewitched
Cesira fading
Daily   daily   feeble   softer

The doctor   Phthisis
The wise woman   says to take her
So we   following her instruction
I and the neighbour
Take her—

The glass rattling
The rain slipping
I and the neighbour and her aunt
Bunched together
And Cesira
Droops across the cab

Fields and houses
Pass   like the pulling out
Of sweetmeat ribbon
From a rascal's mouth
Till

A wheel in a rut
Jerks back my girl on the padding
And the hedges into the sky

Coming to the magic tree

Cesira becomes as a wild beast
                    A tree of age

If Cesira should not become as a wild beast
It is merely Phthisis
This being the wise woman's instruction

Knowing she has to die
We drive home
To wait
She certainly does in time

It is unnatural in a Father
Bewitching a daughter
Whose hair   down   covers her thighs

Three Moments in Paris

I. One O'Clock at Night

Though you had never possessed me
I had belonged to you since the beginning of time
And sleepily I sat on your chair beside you
Leaning against your shoulder
And your careless arm across my back   gesticulated
As your indisputable male voice   roared
Through my brain and my body
Arguing dynamic decomposition
Of which I was understanding nothing
Sleepily
And the only less male voice of your brother pugilist of the
    intellect
Boomed   as it seemed to me   so sleepy
Across an interval of a thousand miles
An interim of a thousand years
But you who make more noise than any man in the world when
    you clear your throat
Deafening   woke me
And I caught the thread of the argument
Immediately assuming my personal mental attitude
And ceased to be a woman

Beautiful half-hour of being a mere woman
The animal woman
Understanding nothing of man
But mastery   and the security of imparted physical heat
Indifferent to cerebral gymnastics
Or regarding them as the self-indulgent play of children
Or the thunder of alien gods
But you woke me up

Anyhow   who am I that I should criticize your theories of
    plastic velocity

"Let us go home   she is tired   and wants to go to bed."

II. *Café du Néant*

Little tapers leaning   lighted diagonally
Stuck in coffin tables of the Café du Néant
Leaning to the breath of baited bodies
Like young poplars fringing the Loire

Eyes that are full of love
And eyes that are full of kohl
Projecting light across the fulsome ambiente
Trailing the rest of the animal behind them
Telling of tales without words
And lies of no consequence
One way or another

The young lovers hermetically buttoned up in black
To black cravat
To the blue powder edge dusting the yellow throat
What color could have been your bodies
When last you put them away

Nostalgic youth
Holding your mistress's pricked finger
In the indifferent flame of the taper
Synthetic symbol of   LIFE
In this factitious chamber of   DEATH
The woman
As usual
Is smiling   as bravely
As it is given to her to be   brave

While the brandy cherries
In winking glasses
Are decomposing
Harmoniously
With the flesh of spectators
And at a given spot
There is one
Who
Having the concentric lighting focussed precisely upon her
Prophetically blossoms in perfect putrefaction
Yet   there are cabs outside the door.

III. Magasins du Louvre

All the virgin eyes in the world are made of glass

Long lines of boxes
Of dolls
Propped against banisters
Walls and pillars
Huddled on shelves
And composite babies with arms extended
Hang from the ceiling
Beckoning
Smiling
In a profound silence
Which the shop walker left trailing behind him
When he ambled to the further end of the gallery
To annoy the shop-girl

All the virgin eyes in the world are made of glass
They alone have the effrontery to
Stare through the human soul
Seeing nothing
Between parted fringes

One cocotte wears a bowler hat and a sham camellia
And one an iridescent boa
For there are two of them
Passing
And the solicitous mouth of one is straight
The other curved to a static smile
They see the dolls
And for a moment their eyes relax
To a flicker of elements unconditionally primeval
And now averted
Seek each other's   surreptitiously
To know if the other has seen
While mine are inextricably entangled with the pattern of the
    carpet
As eyes are apt to be
In their shame
Having surprised a gesture that is ultimately intimate

All the virgin eyes in the world are made of glass.

Sketch of a Man on a Platform

Man of absolute physical equilibrium
You stand so straight on your legs
Every plank or clod you plant your feet on
Becomes roots for those limbs

Among the men you accrete to yourself
You are more heavy
And more light
Force being most equitably disposed
Is easiest to lift from the ground
So at the same time
Your movements
Unassailable
Savor of the airy-fairy of the ballet
The essence of a Mademoiselle Genée
Winks in the to-and-fro of your cuff-links

Your projectile nose
Has meddled in the more serious business
Of the battle-field
With the same incautious aloofness
Of intense occupation
That it snuffles the trail of the female
And the comfortable
Passing odors of love

Your genius
So much less in your brain

Than in your body
Reinforcing the hitherto negligible

Qualities
Of life
Deals so exclusively with
The vital
That it is equally happy expressing itself
Through the activity of pushing
THINGS
In the opposite direction
To that which they are lethargically willing to go
As in the amative language
Of the eyes

Fundamentally unreliable
You leave others their initial strength
Concentrating
On stretching the theoretic elastic of your conceptions
Till the extent is adequate
To the hooking on
Of any— or all
Forms of creative idiosyncracy
While the occasional snap
Of actual production
Stings the face of the public.

Virgins Plus Curtains Minus Dots

Latin Borghese

Houses hold virgins
The door's on the chain

'Plumb streets with hearts'
'Bore curtains with eyes'

Virgins   without dots*
Stare   beyond probability

See the men pass
Their hats are not ours
We   take a walk
They are going somewhere
And they   may look everywhere
Men's eyes   look into things
Our eyes   look out

A great deal of ourselves
We offer to the mirror
Something less to the confessional
The rest   to Time
There is so much   Time
Everything is full of it
               Such a long time

Virgins may whisper
'Transparent nightdresses made all of lace'

*Marriage Portions

Virgins may squeak
'My dear   I should faint'
Flutter . . . . . flutter . . . . flutter . . . .
 . . . . 'And then   the man—'
Wasting our giggles
For we have no dots

We have been taught
Love is a god
White   with soft wings
                    Nobody shouts
          Virgins for sale
Yet where are our coins
For buying a purchaser
Love is a god
                Marriage expensive
A secret well kept
Makes the noise of the world
Nature's arms spread wide
Making room for us
          Room for all of us
Somebody who was never
                          a virgin
Has bolted the door
Put curtains at our windows
See the men pass
They   are going somewhere

Fleshes like weeds
Sprout in the light
So much flesh in the world
                Wanders at will

Some   behind curtains
Throbs to the night
Bait   to the stars

Spread it with gold
And you carry it home
Against your shirt front
To   a shaded light
With the door locked
Against virgins who
Might   scratch

Babies in Hospital

I.

Small Elena
Of shrunken limbs
And ample sex
Who
Having filched
The atrophied
Woman-smile of your mother
Scatter it
On the eating unseen
Tuberculous

Inaudible hands
On the counter-pane
It might have been
Impossible
Fingers should be so long
Being so tiny
But Nature
Needing no microscope
In her laboratory
Found it just as easy
Marshalling imperceptible
Hosts
To bone of your arm
Among overlapping of lint
Attaining a dignity
Unworthy of your years
Two and a half!

II.

Hail to you
Bad little boy
Lying
In bound beauty
Of only a broken leg
And thank you
For throwing
Your bricks on the floor
For the third time
And the smack
You gave me
For the thermometer

Delightfully male
Already gallant
You smooth the mackintosh
For Elena to sit on beside you
Her fragility
Being irresistibly for you
You are very wise
Precocious coquette
Who never learnt to talk
To look at him
Before
Your semi-imbecile
Eyes shut
It is not given to each of us
To be desired.

III.

Tend
Do not touch
Apparent flowers
Of festering secret

And the fly-by-nights
Such little things
I cannot be your mother
There are already
So many ignorances
I am not guilty of.

Giovanni Franchi

The threewomen   who all walked
In   the same dress
And it had falling ferns on it
Skipped parallel
To the progress
Of Giovanni Franchi

Giovanni Franchi's wrists flicked
Flickeringly as he flacked them
His wrists explained things
Infectiously   by way of his adolescence
His adolescence was all there was of him
Whatever was left was rather awkward
His adolescence tuned to the tops of trees
Descended to the fallacious nobility
Of his first pair of trousers

They were tubular   flapped friezily
The colour of coppered mustard
What matter
Were they not the first
No others could ever be the first again
The ferns on the flounces of the threewomen
Began fading as she thought of it
Tea-table problems for insane asylums
Are démodé
Démodé

Allow us to rely on our instincts

The threewomen was composed of three instincts
Each sniffing divergently directed draughts

The first instinct   first again   may
renascent gods save us from the enigmatic
penetralia of Firstness
Was to be faithful to a man   first
The second   to be loyal to herself first
She would have to find which self first
The third which might as well have been first
Was to find out   how many toes   the
philosopher Giovanni Bapini had   first

Giovanni Franchi hooligan-faced and latin-born
You imagine what he looked like
Looked it   as nearly as he could   as the
philosopher looked
His articulations were excellent
Still   where Giovanni Bapini was cymophanous
Giovanni Franchi was merely pale

His acolytian sincerity
The sensitive down among his freckles
Fell in with the patriotic souls of flags
Red white and green flags   filliping piazzas
When the "National Idea" arrived on the Milan Express
He scuttled winsomely
To its distribution from a puffer
For the declaration of War

Continually cutting off an angle from Paszkowski's
Through plate-glass swingings
To look as busy bodily
As the philosopher's brain was
As Giovanni Bapini importuned mobs
From monumental gums
To the sparky detritus
From the hurried cigarette
Of his disciple

Whose papa and mama kept a trattoria
Audaciously squatting right opposite the Pitti Palace
The Pitti Palace however stolid   could hardly help
    noticing
Being an aristocrat it went on looking
As plainly piled up as ever
The Pitti Palace has never been known to mention the trattoria
Or mention Giovanni Franchi
Sitting in it
At a book
It could not see from that distance
Giovanni watching the munchers supporting his parents
With an eye
On assuring himself
Of their sufficient impression
By erudition

He was so young
That explains so much
No book ever explained what to be young is
But they look so much more important for that
Giovanni was in continuous exstacy
Induced by the imposing look of them
When Giovanni Bapini spoke of them
He could not tell
How completely more precious
Would be such knowledge
As how many toes the philosopher Giovanni Bapini had

Now the threewomen
For pity's sake
Let us think of her as she   to save time
Seeing the minor Giovanni
Sitting at the major Giovanni's feet
Made sure he must be counting his toes
All to the contrary   he was picking the philosopher's
    brains

Happy in the security that when he had done
He would still be youthful enough to sort out his own

He listened at the elder's lips
That taught him of earthquakes and women
Of women ─────────────────
His manners were abominable
He would kill a woman
Quite inconspicuously it is true
And neglect to attend her funeral
I mean the older man
And what he told
Giovanni Franchi
About those pernicious persons
Was so extremely good for him
It entirely spoilt his first love-affair
To such an extent   it never came off

We have read of
Trattoria   meaning eating-house
Piazzas   or squares
The Pitti Palace   enormous
And Paszkowski's   for beer
All are in Firenze
Firenze is Florence
Some think it is a woman with flowers in her hair
But NO   it is a city with stones on the streets

Giovanni Bapini often said
Everybody in Firenze knows me
And everybody did
Excepting── That is   she didn't
She never knew what he was
Or how he was himself
Yet she uniquely was the one
To speculate   upon the number of his toes

The days growing longer
Fulfilling her of curiosity

She made a moth's-net
Of metaphor and miracles
And on the incandescent breath of civilizations
She chased by moon-and-morn light
Philosopher's toes

As virginal   as had he never worn them
Clear of 'white marks mean money'
All quicks and cores
They fluttered to her fantasy
Fell into her lap
While she gathered her ferny flounces about them
They inappropriately passed

But Giovanni Franchi was there
He almost winked it at her
That he was there
His eyes were intrepid with phantom secrets
The Philosopher had flung to him
And as she tripped by him
She guessed   these all
All   but the number of those toes

She made diurnal pilgrimage
To the trattoria
To eat
Trout   that might have been trained for circuses
If minarets   grew in miniature whirlpools
And mayonnaise   that helped her to forget
That what is underneath   need never matter

She put all minor riddles out of her
Such as

What was the under-cover of Franchi's book
Telling to the plaid pattern of the table-cloth
Too shy to interrogate
She sent ambassadors
To the disciple
They returned
Oh rats
Quite manifest   that Giovanni Franchi
Some semieffigy
Damned by scholiums
Knew no more   how many toes——
Than   Giovanni Bapini knew himself

At the Door of the House

A thousand women's eyes
Riveted to the unrealisable
Scatter the wash-stand of the card-teller
Defiled marble of Carrara
      On which she spreads
Color-picture maps of destiny
In the corner
of an inconducive bed-room

   "Impassioned
Doubly impassioned
Sad
You see these three cards
But here is the double Victory
And there is an elderly lady
Ill   in whom you are concerned
This   is the Devil
And these two skeletons
Are mortifications
You   are going to make a journey

At evening   about love
Here is the Man of the Heart
Turning his shoulders to a lady
Covered with tears about matrimony

At the door of your house
There is a letter about an affair
And a bed   and a table
And this ace of spades turned upside-down
'With respect'

Means   that some man
Has   well you know
Intentions   little honorable

Here you are   covered with tears
For a deception
The Man of the Heart
Is in thoughtfulness for a letter
He will make a journey at evening
And really   lady
I should say
It will not be long before you see him
For there he is at the door of the house

And look
Here are you
        And here is he
        In life and thought
At the door of the house"

Muddled among the aniline brightness of the Tauro cards

The wheels with wings
The rows on rows of goblets
        Passionate magenta blossoms
Hermits   —bring luck—
Moons   Prison-fortresses
Cudgels
A man cut in half
        Means a deception
And the nude woman
    Stands for the world

    Those eyes

Of Petronilla Lucia Letizia
        Felicita

Filomena Amalia
Orsola Geltrude Caterina Delfina
Zita Bibiana   Tarsilla
Eufemia,
Looking for the little love-tale
That never came true
At the door of the house

The Effectual Marriage

or

THE INSIPID NARRATIVE

of

GINA AND MIOVANNI

The door was an absurd thing
Yet it was passable
They quotidienly passed through it
It was this shape

Gina and Miovanni   who they were God knows
They knew   it was important to them
This being of who they were
They were themselves
Corporeally   transcendentally   consecutively
conjunctively   and they were quite   complete

In the evening they looked out of their two windows
Miovanni out of his library window
Gina from the kitchen window
From among his pots and pans
Where he so kindly kept her
Where she so wisely busied herself
Pots and Pans   she cooked in them
All sorts of sialagogues
Some say   that happy women are immaterial

So here we might dispense with her
Gina being a female
But she was more than that
Being an incipience   a correlative
an instigation of the reaction of man
From the palpable to the transcendent
Mollescent irritant of his fantasy
Gina had her use   Being useful

contentedly conscious
She flowered in Empyrean
From which no well-mated woman ever returns

Sundays   a warm light in the parlor
From the gritty road   on the white wall
anybody could see it
Shimmered a composite effigy
Madonna   crinolined   a man
hidden beneath her hoop
Ho for the blue and red of her
The silent eyelids of her
The shiny smile of her

Ding dong   said the bell
Miovanni   Gina called
Would it be fitting for you to tell
the time for supper
Pooh   said Miovanni   I am
Outside time and space

Patience said Gina   is an attribute
And she learned   at any hour to offer
The dish   appropriately delectable

What had Miovanni made of his ego
In his library
What had Gina wondered   among the pots and pans
One never asked the other
So they   the wise ones   eat their suppers in peace

Of what their peace consisted
We cannot say
Only that he was magnificently man
She insignificantly a woman who understood
Understanding   what is that
To Each   his entity   to others

their idiosyncrasies   to the free expansion
to the annexed   their liberty
To man his work
To woman her love
Succulent meals   and an occasional caress
            So be it
                    It so seldom is

While Miovanni thought alone in the dark
Gina supposed that peeping   she might see
A round light   shining   where his mind was
She never opened the door
Fearing that this might blind her
Or even
That she should see   Nothing at all
So while he thought
She hung out of the window
Watching for falling stars
And when a star fell
She wished   that still
Miovanni would love her to-morrow
And as Miovanni
Never gave any heed to the matter
He did

Gina was a woman
Who wanted everything
To be everything in woman
Everything everyway at once
Diurnally variegate
Miovanni always knew her
She was Gina
Gina who lent monogamy
With her fluctuant aspirations
A changeant consistency
Unexpected intangibilities

Miovanni remained
Monumentally the same
The same Miovanni
If he had become anything else
Gina's world would have been at an end
Gina with no axis to revolve on
Must have dwindled to a full stop

In the mornings she dropped
Cool crystals
Through devotional fingers
Saccharine   for his cup
And marketed
With a Basket
Trimmed with a red flannel flower
When she was lazy
She wrote a poem on the milk bill
The first strophe   Good morning
The second   Good night
Something not too difficult to
Learn by heart

The scrubbed smell of the white-wood table
Greasy cleanliness   of the chopper board
The coloured vegetables
Intuited quality of flour
Crickly sparks of straw-fanned charcoal
Ranged themselves among her audacious happinesses
Pet simplicities of her Universe
Where circles were only round
                    Having no vices.

(This narrative halted when I learned that the
house which inspired it was the home of a mad
woman.
                              —Forte dei Marmi)

Human Cylinders

The human cylinders
Revolving in the enervating dust
That wraps each closer in the mystery
Of singularity
Among the litter of a sunless afternoon
Having eaten without tasting
Talked without communion
And at least two of us
Loved a very little
Without seeking
To know if our two miseries
In the lucid rush-together of automatons
Could form one opulent well-being

Simplifications of men
In the enervating dusk
Your indistinctness
Serves me the core of the kernel of you
When in the frenzied reaching-out of intellect to intellect
Leaning brow to brow   communicative
Over the abyss of the potential
Concordance of respiration
Shames
Absence of corresponding between the verbal sensory
And reciprocity
Of conception
And expression
Where each extrudes beyond the tangible
One thin pale trail of speculation
From among us we have sent out
Into the enervating dusk

One little whining beast
Whose longing
Is to slink back to antediluvian burrow
And one elastic tentacle of intuition
To quiver among the stars

The impartiality of the absolute
Routs   the polemic
Or which of us
Would not
Receiving the holy-ghost
Catch it   and caging
    Lose it
Or in the problematic
Destroy the Universe
With a solution.

The Black Virginity

Baby Priests
On green sward
Yew-closed
Scuttle to sunbeams
Silk beaver
Rhythm of redemption
Fluttering of Breviaries

Fluted black silk cloaks
Hung square from shoulders
Truncated juvenility
Uniform segregation
Union in severity
Modulation
Intimidation
Pride of misapprehended preparation
Ebony statues training for immobility
Anaemic jawed
Wise saw to one another

Prettily the little ones
Gesticulate benignly upon one another in the sun buzz—
Finger and thumb circles postulate pulpits
Profiles forsworn to Donatello
Munching tall talk vestral shop
Evangelical snobs
Uneasy dreaming
In hermetically-sealed dormitories
Not of me or you Sister Saraminta
Of no more or less
Than the fit of Pope's mitres

It is an old religion that put us in our places
Here am I in lilac print
Preposterously no less than the world flesh and devil
Having no more idea what those are
What I am
Than Baby Priests of what "He" is
or they are—
Messianic mites tripping measured latin ring-a-roses
Subjugated adolescence
Retraces loose steps to furling of Breviaries
In broiling shadows
The last with apostolic lurch
Tries for a high hung fruit
And misses
Any way it is inedible
It is always thus
In the Public Garden.

Parallel lines
An old man
Eyeing a white muslin girl's school
And all this
As pleasant as bewildering
Would not eventually meet
I am for ever bewildered
Old men are often grown greedy—
What nonsense
It is noon
And salvation's seedlings
Are headed off for the refectory.

Ignoramus

Shut it up

Sing silence
To destiny
Give half-a-crown
To a magician
Half a glance
To window-eclipse
And count the glumes
Of your day's bargaining
Lying
In the lining
Of your pocket
        While compromising
Between the perpendicular and horizontal
Some other tramp
Leans against
The night-nursery of trams

Puffs of black night
Quiver the neck
Of the Clown of Fortune
        Dribble out of his trouser-ends
In dust-to-dust
Till cock-kingdom-come-crow
You can hear the heart-beating
Accoupling
of the masculine and feminine
Universal principles
Mating
And the martyrdom of morning

Caged with the love of houseflies
The avidity of youth
And incommensuration.

Day-spring
Bursting on repetition
          "My friend the Sun
          You have probably met before"
Or breakfasting on rain
You hurry
To interpolate
The over-growth
Of vegetation
With a walking-stick

Or smear a friend
With a greasy residuum
From boiling your soul down
          You can walk to Empyrean to-gether
Under the same
Oil-silk umbrella

"I must have you
Count stars for me
Out of their numeral excess
Please keep the brightest
For the last

Lions' Jaws

O FAR away on the Benign Peninsular

   .   .   .   .   .

   That automatic fancier of lyrical birds
          Danriel Gabrunzio
with melodious magnolia
perfumes his mise en scène
where impotent neurotics
wince at the dusk

The national arch-angel
loved
several countesses
in a bath full of tuberoses
soothed by the orchestra
at the 'Hotel Majestic Palace'

 .   .   .   the sobbing
from the psycho-pathic wards
of his abandoned harem
purveys amusement for 'High Life'

The comet conquerer
showers upon continental libraries
translated stars   .   .   .
accusations of the alcove
where
with a pomaded complaisance
he trims rococo liaisons   .   .   .
   .   .   .   a tooth-tattoo of an Elvira
into a Maria's flesh

And every noon
bare virgins riding alabaster donkeys
receive Danriel Gabrunzio
from the Adriatic
in a golden bath-towel
signed with the zodiac
in pink chenille

    *   *   *   *

Defiance of old idolatries
inspires new schools
 . . . .

Danriel Gabrunzio's compatriots
concoct new courtships
to intrigue
the myriad-fleshed Mistress
of "the Celebrated"

The antique envious thunder
of Latin littérateurs
rivaling Gabrunzio's satiety
burst in a manifesto
notifying women's wombs
of Man's immediate agamogenesis
 . . .   Insurance
of his spiritual integrity
against the carnivorous courtesan
 . . .   Manifesto
of the flabbergast movement
hurled by the leader Raminetti
to crash upon the audacious lightning
of Gabrunzio's fashions in lechery
 . . . and wheedle its inevitable way
to the "excepted" woman's heart
her cautious pride
extorting betrayal

of Woman wholesale
to warrant her surrender
with a sense of   .   .   .   Victory

Raminetti
cracked the whip of the circus-master
astride a prismatic locomotive
ramping the tottering platform
of the Arts
of which this conjuring commercial traveller
imported some novelties from
Paris in his pocket   .   .   .
souvenirs for his disciples
to flaunt
at his dynamic carnival

The erudite Bapini
experimenting
in auto-hypnotic God-head
on a mountain
rolls off as Raminetti's plastic velocity
explodes his crust
of library dust
and hurrying threatening nakedness
to a vermilion ambush
in flabbergastism
.   .   .   he kisses Raminetti
full on his oratory
in the arena
rather fancying Himself
in the awesome proportions
of an eclectic mother-in-law
to a raw ménage.

Thus academically chaperoned
the flabbergasts
blaze from obscurity

to deny their creed in cosy corners
to every feminine opportunity
and Raminetti
anxious to get a move on this beating-Gabrunzio-business
possesses the women of two generations
except a few
who jump the train at the next station   .   .   .
.   .   .   while the competitive Bapini
publishes a pretty comment
involving woman in the plumber's art
and advertises
his ugliness as an excellent aphrodisiac

*   *   *   *

Shall manoeuvres in the new manner
pass unremarked?
             .   .   .

These amusing men
discover in their mail
duplicate petitions
to be the lurid mother of "their" flabbergast child
from Nima Lyo, alias Anim Yol, alias
Imna Oly
(secret service buffoon to the Woman's Cause)
       .   .   .   .

While flabbergastism boils over
and Ram: and Bap:
avoid each other's sounds
This Duplex-Conquest
claims a "sort of success"
for the Gabrunzio resisters.

Envoi

Raminetti gets short sentences
for obstructing public thoroughfares

Bapini is popular in "Vanity Fair"
As for Imna Oly   .   .   .
I agree with Mrs. Krar Standing Hail
She is not quite a lady.   .   .   .
.   .   .   .   .

Riding the sunset
DANRIEL GABRUNZIO
corrects
the lewd precocity
of Raminetti and Bapini
with his sonorous violation of Fiume
and drops his eye
into the fatal lap
of Italy.

II

SONGS TO JOANNES

(1917)

Songs to Joannes

I

Spawn of Fantasies
Silting the appraisable
Pig Cupid   his rosy snout
Rooting erotic garbage
"Once upon a time"
Pulls a weed   white star-topped
Among wild oats   sown in mucous-membrane

I would   an   eye in a Bengal light
Eternity in a sky-rocket
Constellations in an ocean
Whose rivers run no fresher
Than a trickle of saliva

These   are suspect places

I must live in my lantern
Trimming subliminal flicker
Virginal   to the bellows
Of Experience
                              Coloured   glass

II

                         The skin-sack
In which a wanton duality
Packed
All the completion of my infructuous impulses
Something the shape of a man
To the casual vulgarity of the merely observant

More of a clock-work mechanism
Running down against time
To which I am not paced
    My finger-tips are numb from fretting your hair
A God's door-mat
                On the threshold of your mind

III

We might have coupled
In the bed-ridden monopoly of a moment
Or broken flesh with one another
At the profane communion table
Where wine is spill'd on promiscuous lips

We might have given birth to a butterfly
With the daily news
Printed in blood on its wings

IV

Once in a mezzanino
The starry ceiling
Vaulted an unimaginable family
Bird-like abortions
With human throats
And Wisdom's eyes
Who wore lamp-shade red dresses
And woolen hair

One bore a baby
In a padded porte-enfant
Tied with a sarsenet ribbon
To her goose's wings

But for the abominable shadows
I would have lived

Among their fearful furniture
To teach them to tell me their secrets
Before I guessed
—Sweeping the brood clean out

V

Midnight empties the street
Of all but us
Three
I am undecided which way back
                    To the left a boy
—One wing has been washed in the rain
    The other will never be clean any more—
Pulling door-bells to remind
Those that are snug
                    To the right a haloed ascetic
                    Threading houses
Probes wounds for souls
—The poor can't wash in hot water—
And I don't know which turning to take
Since you got home to yourself—first

VI

I know the Wire-Puller intimately
And if it were not for the people
On whom you keep one eye
You could look straight at me
And Time would be set back

VII

My pair of feet
Smack the flag-stones
That are something left over from your walking
The wind stuffs the scum of the white street

Into my lungs and my nostrils
Exhilarated birds
Prolonging flight into the night
Never reaching— — — — — — —

VIII

I am the jealous store-house of the candle-ends
That lit your adolescent learning
— — — — — — — — — —

Behind God's eyes
There might
Be other lights

IX

When we lifted
Our eye-lids on Love
A cosmos
Of coloured voices
And laughing honey

And spermatozoa
At the core of Nothing
In the milk of the Moon

X

Shuttle-cock and battle-door
A little pink-love
And feathers are strewn

XI

Dear one   at your mercy
Our Universe
Is only

A colorless onion
You derobe
Sheath by sheath
        Remaining
A disheartening odour
About your nervy hands

XII

Voices break on the confines of passion
Desire   Suspicion   Man   Woman
Solve in the humid carnage

Flesh from flesh
Draws the inseparable delight
Kissing at gasps   to catch it

Is it true
That I have set you apart
Inviolate in an utter crystallization
Of all   the jolting of the crowd
Taught me willingly to live to share

Or are you
Only the other half
Of an ego's necessity
Scourging pride with compassion
To the shallow sound of dissonance
And boom of escaping breath

XIII

Come to me   There is something
I have got to tell you   and I can't tell
Something taking shape
Something that has a new name
A new dimension

A new use
A new illusion

It is ambient   And it is in your eyes
Something shiny   Something only for you
                     Something that I must not see

It is in my ears   Something very resonant
Something that you must not hear
                     Something only for me

Let us be very jealous
Very suspicious
Very conservative
Very cruel
Or we might make an end of the jostling of aspirations
Disorb inviolate egos

Where two or three are welded together
They shall become god
— — — — — — —
Oh that's right
Keep away from me   Please give me a push
Don't let me understand you   Don't realise me
Or we might tumble together
Depersonalized
Identical
Into the terrific Nirvana
Me you — you — me

XIV

Today
Everlasting   passing   apparent   imperceptible
To you
I bring the nascent virginity of
—Myself   for the moment

No love   or the other thing
Only the impact of lighted bodies
Knocking sparks off each other
In chaos

XV

Seldom   Trying for Love
Fantasy dealt them out as gods
Two or three men   looked only human

But you alone
Superhuman   apparently
I had to be caught in the weak eddy
Of your drivelling humanity
                    To love you most

XVI

We might have lived together
In the lights of the Arno
Or gone apple stealing under the sea
Or played
Hide and seek in love and cob-webs
And a lullaby on a tin-pan

And   talked till there were no more tongues
To talk with
And never have known any better

XVII

I don't care
Where the legs of the legs of the furniture are walking to
Or what is hidden in the shadows they stride
Or what would look at me
If the shutters were not shut

Red   a warm colour on the battle-field
Heavy on my knees as a counterpane
Count counter
I counted   the fringe of the towel
Till two tassels clinging together
Let the square room fall away
From a round vacuum
Dilating with my breath

XVIII

Out of the severing
Of hill from hill
The interim
Of star from star
The nascent
Static
Of night

XIX

Nothing so conserving
As cool cleaving
Note of the Q H U
Clear carving
Breath-giving
Pollen smelling
Space

White telling
Of slaking
Drinkable
Through fingers
Running water
Grass haulms
Grow to

Leading astray
Of fireflies
Aerial quadrille
Bouncing
Off one another
Again conjoining
In recaptured pulses
Of light

You too
Had something
At that time
Of a green-lit glow-worm
— — — — — — —
Yet slowly drenched
To raylessness
In rain

XX

Let Joy go solace-winged
To flutter whom she may concern

XXI

I store up nights against you
Heavy with shut-flower's nightmares
— — — — — — — — — —
Stack noons
Curled to the solitaire
Core of the
Sun

XXII

Green things grow
Salads

For the cerebral
Forager's revival
Upon bossed bellies
Of mountains
Rolling in the sun
And flowered flummery
Breaks
To my silly shoes

In ways without you
I go
Gracelessly
As things go

XXIII

Laughter in solution
Stars in a stare
Irredeemable pledges
Of pubescent consummations
Rot
To the recurrent moon
Bleach
To the pure white
Wickedness of pain

XXIV

The procreative truth of Me
Petered out
In pestilent
Tear drops
Little lusts and lucidities
And prayerful lies
Muddled with the heinous acerbity
Of your street-corner smile

XXV

Licking the Arno
The little rosy
Tongue of Dawn
Interferes with our eyelashes
— — — — — — — —

We twiddle to it
Round and round
Faster
And turn into machines

Till the sun
Subsides in shining
Melts some of us
Into abysmal pigeon-holes
Passion has bored
In warmth

Some few of us
Grow to the level of cool plains
Cutting our foot-hold
With steel eyes

XXVI

Shedding our petty pruderies
From slit eyes

We sidle up
To Nature
— — — that irate pornographist

XXVII

Nucleus   Nothing
Inconceivable concept

Insentient repose
The hands of races
Drop off from
Immodifiable plastic

The contents
Of our ephemeral conjunction
In aloofness from Much
Flowed to approachment of — — — —
NOTHING
There was a man and a woman
In the way
While the Irresolvable
Rubbed with our daily deaths
Impossible eyes

XXVIII

The steps go up for ever
And they are white
And the first step   is the last white
Forever
Coloured   conclusions
Smelt   to synthetic
Whiteness
Of my
Emergence
And I am burnt quite white
In the climacteric
Withdrawal of your sun
And wills and words all white
Suffuse
Illimitable monotone

White   where there is nothing to see
But a white towel
Wipes the cymophanous sweat

—Mist rise of living—
From your
Etiolate body
And the white dawn
Of your   New Day
Shuts down on me

Unthinkable   that white over there
— — — Is smoke from your house

XXIX

Evolution   fall foul of
Sexual equality
Prettily miscalculate
Similitude

Unnatural selection
Breed such sons and daughters
As shall jibber at each other
Uninterpretable cryptonyms
Under the moon

Give them some way of braying brassily
For caressive calling
Or to homophonous hiccoughs
Transpose the laugh
Let them suppose that tears
Are snowdrops or molasses
Or anything
Than human insufficiencies
Begging dorsal vertebrae

Let meeting be the turning
To the antipodean
And Form   a blurr
Anything

Than seduce them
To the one
As simple satisfaction
For the other

Let them clash together
From their incognitoes
In seismic orgasm

For far further
Differentiation
Rather than watch
Own-self distortion
Wince in the alien ego

XXX

In some
Prenatal plagiarism
Fœtal buffoons
Caught tricks
— — — — —

From archetypal pantomime
Stringing emotions
Looped aloft
— — — —

For the blind eyes
That Nature knows us with
And the most of Nature   is green
— — — — — — — — — —

What guaranty
For the proto-form
We fumble

Our souvenir ethics to
— — — — — — —

XXXI

Crucifixion
Of a busy-body
Longing to interfere so
With the intimacies
Of your insolent isolation

Crucifixion
Of an illegal ego's
Eclosion
On your equilibrium
Caryatid   of an idea

Crucifixion
Wracked arms
Index extremities
In vacuum
To the unbroken fall

XXXII

The moon is cold
Joannes
Where the Mediterranean — — — — —

XXXIII

The prig of passion — — — —
To your professorial paucity

Proto-plasm was raving mad
Evolving us — — —

XXXIV

Love — — — the preeminent litterateur

III

CORPSES AND GENIUSES

(POEMS 1919–1930)

Passport photo of Loy, 1920s

O Hell

To clear the drifts of spring
Of our forebear's excrements
And bury the subconscious archives
Under unaffected flowers

    Indeed—

Our person is a covered entrance to infinity
Choked with the tatters of tradition

Goddesses and Young Gods
Caress the sanctity of Adolescence
In the shaft of the sun.

The Dead

We have flowed out of ourselves
Beginning on the outside
That shrivable skin
Where you leave off

Of infinite elastic
Walking the ceiling
Our eyelashes polish stars

Curled close in the youngest corpuscle
Of a descendant
We spit up our passions in our grand-dams

Fixing the extension of your reactions
Our shadow lengthens
In your fear

You are so old
Born in our immortality
Stuck fast as Life
In one impalpable
Omniprevalent Dimension

We are turned inside out
Your cities lie digesting in our stomachs
Street lights footle in our ocular darkness

Having swallowed your irate hungers
Satisfied before bread-breaking
To your dissolution
We splinter into Wholes

Stirring the remorses of your tomorrow
Among the refuse of your unborn centuries
In our busy ashbins
Stink the melodies
Of your
So easily reducible
Adolescences

Our tissue is of that which escapes you
Birth-Breaths and orgasms
The shattering tremor of the static
The far-shore of an instant
The unsurpassable openness of the circle
Legerdemain of God

Only in the segregated angles of Lunatic Asylums
Do those who have strained to exceeding themselves
Break on our edgeless contours

The mouthed echoes of what
Has exuded to our companionship
Is horrible to the ear
Of the half that is left inside them.

Mexican Desert

The belching ghost-wail of the locomotive
trailing her rattling wooden tail
into the jazz-band sunset.   .   .   .

The mountains in a row
set pinnacles of ferocious isolation
under the alien hot heaven

Vegetable cripples of drought
thrust up the parching appeal
cracking open the earth
stump-fingered cacti
and hunch-back palm trees
belabour the cinders of twilight.   .   .   .

Perlun

            the whipper snapper child of the sun
His pert blonde spirit
            scoured by the Scandinavian Boreas
His head
            an adolescent oval
            ostrich egg
The victorious   silly   beauty of his face
            awakens to his instincts

A vivacious knick-knack tipped with gold
            he puts the world
            to the test of intuition

            Smiling from ear to ear
            Living from other hands to mouth

            Holding in immaculate arms
                        the syphilitic sailor
                        on his avoided death bunk
                        or the movie vamp
            among the muffled shadows of the shrubberies——

            Picking lemons in Los Angeles   broke

The education of "Prince Fils à Papa"
                        How low men die
                        How women love—
                        The rituals of Dempsey and Carpentier

PERLUN
            asks "Do these flappers of the millionaires
                        think I'm a doll for anyone to pat?"

Poe

a lyric elixir of death

   embalms
   the spindle spirits of your hour glass loves
                           on moon spun nights

sets
    icicled canopy
    for corpses of poesy
    with roses and northern lights

   Where frozen nightingales in ilix aisles

              sing burial rites

Apology of Genius

Ostracized as we are with God—
    The watchers of the civilized wastes
    reverse their signals on our track

    Lepers of the moon
    all magically diseased
    we come among you
    innocent
    of our luminous sores

    unknowing
    how perturbing lights
    our spirit
    on the passion of Man
    until you turn on us your smooth fools' faces
    like buttocks bared in aboriginal mockeries

    We are the sacerdotal clowns
    who feed upon the wind and stars
    and pulverous pastures of poverty

    Our wills are formed
    by curious disciplines
    beyond your laws

    You may give birth to us
    or marry us
    the chances of your flesh
    are not our destiny—

The cuirass of the soul
still shines—
And we are unaware
if you confuse
such brief
corrosion with possession

In the raw caverns of the Increate
we forge the dusk of Chaos
to that imperious jewellery of the Universe
   —the Beautiful—

While to your eyes
      A delicate crop
of criminal mystic immortelles
stands to the censor's scythe.

Brancusi's Golden Bird

The toy
become the aesthetic archetype

As if

some patient peasant God
had rubbed and rubbed
the Alpha and Omega
of Form
into a lump of metal

A naked orientation
unwinged   unplumed
    —the ultimate rhythm
has lopped the extremities
of crest and claw
from
the nucleus of flight

The absolute act
of art
conformed
to continent sculpture
—bare as the brow of Osiris—
this breast of revelation

an incandescent curve
licked by chromatic flames
in labyrinths of reflections

This gong
of polished hyperaesthesia

shrills with brass
as the aggressive light
strikes
its significance

The immaculate
conception
of the inaudible bird
occurs
in gorgeous reticence . . .

Lunar Baedeker

A silver Lucifer
serves
cocaine in cornucopia

To some somnambulists
of adolescent thighs
draped
in satirical draperies

Peris in livery
prepare
Lethe
for posthumous parvenues

Delirious Avenues
lit
with the chandelier souls
of infusoria
from Pharoah's tombstones

lead
to mercurial doomsdays
Odious oasis
in furrowed phosphorous— — —

the eye-white sky-light
white-light district
of lunar lusts

— — — Stellectric signs
"Wing shows on Starway"
"Zodiac carrousel"

Cyclones
of ecstatic dust
and ashes whirl
crusaders
from hallucinatory citadels
of shattered glass
into evacuate craters

A flock of dreams
browse on Necropolis

From the shores
of oval oceans
in the oxidized Orient

Onyx-eyed Odalisques
and ornithologists
observe
the flight
of Eros obsolete

And "Immortality"
mildews . . .
in the museums of the moon

"Nocturnal cyclops"
"Crystal concubine"
— — — — — — —

Pocked with personification
the fossil virgin of the skies
waxes and wanes— — — —

Der Blinde Junge

The dam Bellona
littered
her eyeless offspring
Kreigsopfer
upon the pavements of Vienna

Sparkling precipitate
the spectral day
involves
the visionless obstacle

this slow blind face
pushing
its virginal nonentity
against the light

Pure purposeless eremite
of centripetal sentience

Upon the carnose horologe of the ego
the vibrant tendon index moves not

since the black lightning desecrated
the retinal altar

Void and extinct
this planet of the soul
strains from the craving throat
in static flight upslanting

A downy youth's snout
nozzling the sun
drowned in dumbfounded instinct

Listen!
illuminati of the coloured earth
How this expressionless "thing"
blows out damnation and concussive dark

Upon a mouth-organ

Crab-Angel

An atomic sprite
perched on a polished
    monster-stallion
reigns over Ringling's   revolving
trinity   of circus attractions

Something the contour
of a captured crab
waving its useless pearly claws

From a squat body
pigmy arms
and bow legs
with their baroque calves
curve in a bi-circular attitude
to a ballerina's exstacy

An effigy of Christmas Eves
smile-cast among chrysanthemum curls
it seems a sugar angel
while from a rose flecked ruff of gauze
its manly legs
stamp   on the vast rump of the horse

An iridescent speck
dripped from a rainbow
onto an ebony cloud

Crab-Angel   I christen you
minnikin of masquerade sex

Helen of Lilliput?
Hercules in a powder puff?

SONG

"Had you been born
in regions of the Unicorn
To balance on his ivory horn
perhaps — — —"
"Per Bacco!   'Tis an idiot dwarf
hooked to a wire to make him jump"

Automaton bare-back rider
the circus-master
jerks
your invisible pendulence
from an over-head pulley
to your illusory
leaps in up-a-loft

signs
the horse
racing the orchestra
in rushing show
throw
his whimsy wire-hung dominator

to dart
through circus skies of arc-lit dust
Crab-Angel   like a swimming star

clutching the tail-end of the Chimera
An aerial acrobat
floats on the coiling lightning
of the whirligig

lifts
to the elated symmetry of Flight — — —

A startled rose
whirls in the chaos of the hoofs

The jeering jangling
jazz
crashes to silence

The dwarf—
subsides like an ironic sigh
to the soft earth
and ploughs
his bow-legged way
laboriously   towards the exit
waving a yellow farewell with his perruque

Joyce's Ulysses

The Normal Monster
sings in the Green Sahara

The voice and offal
of the image of God

make Celtic noises
in these lyrical hells

Hurricanes
of reasoned musics
reap the uncensored earth

The loquent consciousness
of living things
pours in torrential languages

The elderly colloquists
the Spirit and the Flesh
are out of tongue — — —

The Spirit
is impaled upon the phallus

Phœnix
of Irish fires
lighten the Occident

with Ireland's wings
flap pandemoniums
of Olympian prose

and satirize
the imperial Rose
of Gaelic perfumes
—England
the sadistic mother
embraces Erin—

Master
of meteoric idiom
present

The word made flesh
and feeding upon itself
with erudite fangs
The sanguine
introspection of the womb

Don Juan
of Judea
upon a pilgrimage
to the Libido

The Press — — —
purring
its lullabyes to sanity

Christ capitalised
scourging
incontrite usurers of destiny
—in hole and corner temples

And hang
the soul's advertisements
outside the ecclesiast's Zoo

A gravid day
spawns

guttural gargoyles
upon the Tower of Babel

Empyrean emporium
where the
rejector—recreator
       Joyce
flashes the giant reflector
on the sub rosa — — —

"The Starry Sky"
OF WYNDHAM LEWIS

who raised
these rocks of human mist

pyramidical survivors
in the cyclorama of space

In the
austere theatre of the Infinite
        the ghosts of the stars
perform the "Presence"

Their celibate shadows
fall
upon the aged radiance
of suns and moons

— The nerves of Heaven
    flinching
    from the antennæ
    of the intellect
— the rays
    that pierce
    the nocturnal heart
The airy eyes of angels
the sublime
experiment in pointillism
faded away

The celestial conservatories
blooming with light
are all blown out

Enviable immigrants
into the pure dimension
immune   serene
devourers of the morning stars of Job

Jehovah's seven days
err in your silent entrails
of geometric Chimeras

The Nirvanic snows
drift — — —
to sky worn images

Marble

Greece has thrown   white shadows
sown
their eyeballs with oblivion

A flock of stone
Gods
perched upon pedestals

A populace
of athlete lilies
of the galleries

scoop the facades of space
with spiral curves
of idol substance
in the silence

A colonnade
Apollo haunts Apollo
with the shade
of a lost hand

Gertrude Stein

Curie
of the laboratory
of vocabulary
　　she crushed
the tonnage
of consciousness
congealed to phrases
　　to extract
a radium of the word

The Widow's Jazz

The white flesh quakes to the negro soul
Chicago! Chicago!

An uninterpretable wail
stirs in a tangle of pale snakes

to the lethargic ecstasy of steps
backing into primeval goal

White man quit his actin' wise
colored folk hab de moon in dere eyes

Haunted by wind instruments
in groves of grace

the maiden saplings
slant to the oboes

and shampooed gigolos
prowl to the sobbing taboos.

An electric crown
crashes the furtive cargoes of the floor.

the pruned contours
dissolve
in the brazen shallows of dissonance
revolving mimes

of the encroaching Eros
in adolescence

The black brute-angels
in their human gloves
bellow through a monstrous growth of metal trunks

and impish musics
crumble the ecstatic loaf
before a swooning flock of doves.

Cravan
colossal absentee
the substitute dark
rolls to the incandescent memory

of love's survivor
on this rich suttee

seared by the flames of sound
the widowed urn

holds impotently
your murdered laughter

Husband
how secretly you cuckold me with death

while this cajoling jazz
blows with its tropic breath

among the echoes of the flesh
a synthesis
of racial caress

The seraph and the ass
in this unerring esperanto
of the earth
converse

of everlit delight

as my desire
receded
to the distance of the dead

searches
the opaque silence
of unpeopled space.

Lady Laura in Bohemia

Trained in a circus of swans
she
proceeds recedingly

Her eliminate flesh of fashion
inseparable from the genealogical tree

columns such towering reticence
of lifted chin
her hiccoughs seem
preparatory to bowing to the Queen

Her somersault descent
into the half-baked underworld
nor the inebriate regret

disturb
her vertical caste
"They drove 'em from the cradle on the curb"

This abbess-prostitute
presides
Jazz-Mass

the gin-fizz eucharist dispenses
—she kisses and curses
in the inconsummate embraces
of a one armed Pittsburger
"Here zip along out of that, Laura!"

"I can't come to Armenonville with you-u
I want to stay here and behave like a grue-u"

Her hell is
Zelli's

Where she floods the bar
with all her curls
in the delirious tears from those bill-poster eyes
plastering 'court proceedings' on the wall
of her inconsiderable soul

A tempered tool
of an exclusive finishing-school
her velvet larynx
slushes

"Glup—you mustn't speak to me
I'm bad—haven't you heard?
I'm Orful—o—g'lup I'm Horrid"

She gushes
"——know young Detruille?
Isn't he di-vi-ne
Such a sweet nature
that boy has

The other night when he tucked in with me
we talked most seriously
we have the same ideals
My dear he has
the eyes of Buddha
O I think he's simply di-vi-ne
The only man who ever understood
everything—   If I'd liked
he would'a'

married me
O I think he's simply di-vi-ne"

Out of the sentimental slobber
Lady Laura—momentarily sober
"How queer—that Detruille
said that he
once was introduced—
Well, I do wonder
how on earth ever such a bounder
happened to meet *my people*"

Sobs on my shoulder—
the memorable divorcée
and christened by the archbishop of Canterbury
Sixteen co-re—
Well let that pass!

She is yet like a diamond on a heap of broken glass.

The Mediterranean Sea

The monstrous sapphire
      lies in her lavish dowry
Crowned by Casinos
set with Provençal
olives
and spears to the mistral

The prevalent Fair
draws idle tides
over volcanic privacies
frilled with the rouse and hush of drowsing foam

Jewelled on her Adriatic arm
Venice, sarcophagus of sighs
and ghostly merchandise,
Splinters on the opal angle of the sun
and dies to the Angelus

an over purpled peach
swarmed by the flies of dusk

From the green incline
of vengence
the Vesuvian vine
drips lucently
Lacrimae Christi
to drift   imperceptibly
with the lost sob of Shelley

Hewn in the Apuane
Carrara stands
as marble sentinel

beyond the blazing rust
of branches
roofing amphibian babies

as they rise

from the Ligurian gullies
Their polished thighs
armoured with aqueous ashes
of the tinselled sands.

Nancy Cunard

Your eyes diffused with holly lights
of ancient Christmas
helmeted with masks
whose silken nostrils
point the cardinal airs,

The vermilion wall
receding as a sin
beyond your moonstone whiteness,

Your chiffon voice
tears with soft mystery
a lily loaded with a sucrose dew
of vigil carnival,

Your lone fragility
of mythological queens
conjures long-vanished dragons —
— their vast jaws
yawning in disillusion,

Your drifting hands
faint as exotic snow
spread silver silence

as a fondant nun
framed in the facing profiles
of Princess Murat
and George Moore

Jules Pascin

So this is death
to rise to the occasion
a shadow
to a shadowy persuasion

Pascin has passed
with his affectionate swagger
his air
of the Crown in the role of jester.

The side-long derby-slanted Bulgar
cocked his jet eye
in its immaculate leer,
and as a coin,
tossed his destiny

Once a shy ivory boy,
the colour of life
had deepened on his cheek
in a wry irony

Pascin has ceased
to flush with ineffaceable bruises
his innubile Circes

Ceased to dangle
demi-rep angels
in tinsel bordels

Silence bleeds

from his slashed wrists
the dim homunculus
within
cries for the unbirth

The seeds
of his sly spirit
are cast to posterity
in satyric squander

a pigeon-toed populace
whose changeling women
jostle the prodigal son
as swine
Cinderellas awander.

IV

COMPENSATIONS OF POVERTY

(POEMS 1942–1949)

Loy in the 1950s

On Third Avenue

"You should have disappeared years ago"—

so disappear
on Third Avenue
to share the heedless incognito

of shuffling shadow-bodies
animate with frustration

whose silence'   only potence is
respiration
preceding the eroded bronze contours
of their other aromas

through the monstrous air
of this red-lit thoroughfare.

Here and there
saturnine
neon-signs
set afire
a feature
on their hueless overcast
of down-cast countenances.

For their ornateness
Time, the contortive tailor,
on and off,
clowned with sweat-sculptured cloth
to press

upon these irreparable dummies
an eerie undress
of mummies
half unwound.

2

Such are the compensations of poverty,
to see————

Like an electric fungus
sprung from its own effulgence
of intercircled jewellery
reflected on the pavement,

like a reliquary sedan-chair,
out of a legend, dumped there,

before a ten-cent Cinema,

a sugar-coated box-office
enjail a Goddess
aglitter, in her runt of a tower,
with ritual claustrophobia.

Such are compensations of poverty,
to see————

Transient in the dust,
the brilliancy
of a trolley
loaded with luminous busts;

lovely in anonymity
they vanish
with the mirage
of their passage.

Mass-Production on 14th Street

Ocean in flower
of closing hour

Pedestrian ocean
of whose undertow,
the rosy scissors of hosiery
snip space
to a triangular racing lace

in an iris circus of Industry.

As a commodious bee
the eye
gathers the infinite facets
of the unique unlikeness
of faces;
the diamond flesh of adolescence
sloping toward perception:

flower over flower,
corollas of complexion
craning from hanging-gardens
of the garment-worker.

All this Eros' produce
dressed in audacious
fuschia,
orgies of orchid
or dented dandelion
among a foliage of mass-production:

carnations
tossed at a carnal caravan
for Carnevale.

The consumer,
the statue of a daisy in her hair
jostles her auxiliary creator
the sempstress—on her hip
a tulip—
horticulture
of her hand-labor.

From the conservatories of commerce'
long glass aisles,
idols of style
project a chic paralysis
through mirrored opals
imaging
the cyclamen and azure
of their mobile simulacra's
tidal passing;

while an ironic
furrier, in the air,
combines the live and static
Femina
of the thoroughfare;

a windowed carousel
of girls revolving
idly in an unconcern
of walking dolls
letting their little wrists from under
the short furs of summer.
jolt to their robot turn.

Now, in the sedative descent of dusk
the street returns to stone;
alone
two lovers, crushed
together in their sweet conjecture
as to Fashion's humour,
point at the ecru and ivory
replica of the dress she has on,
doused in a reservoir of ruby neon;

only — — her buttons are clothespins
the mannequin's, harlequins.

Idiot Child on a Fire-Escape

Obedient as a bundle,
parked in your careful shawls,

you will not fall
into the exertions
of the earth under you,

having spilled,
on your way to becoming,
your skill in Being.

Sunlight excessively
illumines your deep eyelids

domed awnings
over the somnolent
reluctance of your sight—

inverted cups
of mortal ivory,
almost emptied.

Aid of the Madonna

Madonnas are everlastingly mothers in ecstacy.
Their alcove arms
retire the Felicity of their conception
from eld and the disorderliness
of peril,
reproving harm.

Madonnas are æon-moments of motherhood
—a moment is Time surrounded by itself—
in perpetuation of the beatitude,
their attitude
of smiling havens,
of sacred shelves.

Omitted omen of Calvary!
Uncarved Crucifixion!

Madonnas are islands in memory
for earthly mothers, who having begotten,
in early security, heroes of the skies,
on forsaken knees
crave for a moment it be forgotten

that skies once ovational
with celestial oboes
for the Heavenly Celebrities

are skies in clamour
of deathly celerities,
the horror
of diving obituaries
under flowers of fire.

Ephemerid

The Eternal is sustained by serial metamorphosis,
even so Beauty is

metamorphosis surprises!

Low in shadow
of the El's
arboreal iron

some aerial, unbeknown
eerie-form
of dual mobility,

having long wing, an unbelievable
imp-fly

soars

trailing
a horizontal gauze;

trudges, urges,
crouches;

its knees' apexes, a roach's.

Humanly sized
a magnified imago

towing in twofold progress
nameless nostalgia through slush,
enigma along gloom.

As always, has a wisp of whiteness loveliness
to lift the eyelids;
to whisper of subvisual resources
in the uncolor of the unknown.

Across indefinite curbstones
focus
this creature of fictitious
faery,
this eccentric of traffic:

after all
the illicit insect
is only
a little girl—

—a long white muslin curtain,
tied to her pull-over,
afloat from her,
she pilots an ideal load

taking a heavy child
for a ride

in a fragile,
stalling
doll's perambulator.

The dilating wing
billows from her shoulders
the wondering of windows,

mildews, as the soul does,
penury
with dream.

Ponder this
metamorphosis:

Infancy's
kidnap into Fantasia.

Chiffon Velours

She is sere.

Her features,
verging on a shriek
reviling age,

flee from death in odd directions
somehow retained by a web of wrinkles.

The site of vanished breasts
is marked by a safety-pin.

Rigid
at rest against the corner-stone
of a department store.

Hers alone to model
the last creation,

original design
of destitution.

Clothed in memorial scraps
skimpy even for a skeleton.

Trimmed with one sudden burst
of flowery cotton
half her black skirt
glows as a soiled mirror;
reflects the gutter—
a yard of chiffon velours.

Property of Pigeons

Pigeons doze,
or rouse
their striped crescendos
of grey rainbow

a living frieze on the shallow
sill of a factory window.

Pigeons arise,
alight
on vertical bases
of civic brick

whitened with avalanches
of their innocent excrements
as if an angel had been sick;

all that is shown to us
of bird-economies,
financeless,
inobvious as the disposal
of their corpses.

Pigeons make irritant, alluring
music;
quilled solfeggios
of shrill wings winnowing
their rejoicing, cooing
fanaticism for wooing.

Their dolce voices
dotage.

Too and fro, frowardly they live
burnishing each other's
gorgeous halters
in the feathery drive

of preliminaries
to their marriages.

Pigeons disappear,
their claws, a coral landing-gear,
dive for the altar-stair
to their privacies—

a slice of concrete
fallen on a cornice
leading into darkness;
the slit adjacence of houses

where the caressive dusts,
the residue of furnaces
upholster the gossamer
festoons of intestate spiders
for nuptial furniture

Pigeons through some conjurous procedure

appear to reappear
upon the altar-stair
at startling instants
in the immature
torsos of their giant infants;

timid and unflown
stark of plume
naive in nativity
to peer into a vast transparency.

Photo After Pogrom

Arrangement by rage
of human rubble

the false-eternal statues of the slain
until they putrify.

Tossed on a pile of dead,
one woman,
her body hacked to utter beauty
oddly by murder,

attains the absolute smile
of dispossession:

the marble pause before the extinct haven
Death's drear
erasure of fear,

the unassumed
composure

the purposeless peace
sealing the faces
of corpses—

Corpses are virgin.

Time-Bomb

The   present   moment
is   an   explosion   ,
a   scission
of   past   and   future

leaving
those   valorous   disreputables   ,
the   ruins   ,

sentinels
in   an   unknown   dawn
strewn   with   prophecy   .

Only   the   momentary
goggle   of   death
fixes   the   fugitive
momentum   .

Omen of Victory

Women in uniform

relaxed for tea

under a shady garden tree

discover

a dove's feather

fallen in the sugar.

Film-Face

As the Gods sat on Olympus
above travail of clouds

it dominates the garbage-barge
loaded with clouds
of sanitation's chaos;

the enduring face of,
the ruined body of,
the poor people

on Marie Dressler.

Faun Fare

Surreptitious fanfare
of unadams
amingle with ouradams

a seemingly uniform guesthood
met in unsolemn sociability

the amiable scuffle
of cocktail party.

Hooveless fauns
their goat-haunch
discard to antiquity
their hairiness
woven to our worsted.

Most smiles are similes
some
almost imperceptibly
simper to mystery—

As were the tail of the eye
lidded with unlisted likings
on ocular trail
of invitation
to untypical trysts

As were the tail of the eye
feeling for fallacious Foci
a Flitting tongue
licking its luminous chops

o'er tit-bits of other tastes
undue

to the apple
the devil
delivered to Eve.

Neo-Fauns

Whom no forestal feminae
need flee

Altered is the prey.
Of priceless use to civilization

You faun
are balm

to night-club addict
undercover-virgin

for whom
Adonis as escort
—obliging her prestige
as cosmetics her cheek—
is a must.

Faun in you
may she trust
to stage no thrust
of Sabine rape
behind the chauffeur's back

O unisex
Black marketing Amor

with your intermuscular caress
of wrestling entry
to Felicity's
unsentinelled
Arcana.

Your something-for-nothing
Variance
to infertile "Sin."

You
dual yet single
Votaries of Venuseros

As in Athens
So in Manhattan
Erosvenus evoes
his-her worshipper

or whispers

Eros is ours
for is not
Eros
forever overall
a male?

Or implores
for fauns' ease.

Quiet please!
As mondial calliopes
Blaring the bisexual norm
foment the Fauns'
allergy to diapers.

Letters of the Unliving

The present implies presence
thus
unauthorized by the present
these letters are left authorless—
have lost all origin
since the inscribing hand
lost life — — —

The hoarseness of the past
creaks
from creased leaves
covered with unwritten writing
since death's erasure
of the writer — — —
of the lover — — —

Well chosen and so ill-relinquished
the husband heartsease
acme of communion

who made euphonious
our esoteric universe
Ego's oasis
in the sole companion.

As erst my body and my reason
you left to the drought of your dying:
the longing and the lack
when the racked creature
shouted

to an unanswering hiatus
"reunite us"

— — — till slyly — — soporose
patience creeps up on passion.

while the exhilarance of youth
dwindles until out of season
and agony
ends in an equal grave
with ecstasy.

An uneasy mist
rises from this calligraphy of recollection

your documented terror of dementia
due to some merely earthly absence

This package of ago
creaks with the horror of echo
out of void

the bloom of beloving
decoyed
to decay, by the finger
of Hazard the swindler

The deathly handler
left no post-mortem mask — — —
only a callous earth made mouldy
your face excelling Adonis

Posing the extreme enigma
in my Bewilderness

Can whom has ceased to be
Ever have had existence

No longer any you as addresser
there is no addressee
to dally with defunct reality

Can one who still has being
be inexistent?

I am become
dumb
in answer
to your dead language of amor

Diminuendo
of life's imposture
implies no possible retrial
By my so now-while self
of my cloud-corpse
Beshadowing your shroud

the one I was with you
inhumed in chasms,
craters torn by atomic emotion
among chaos

No creator
reconstrues scar-tissue
to shine as birth-star.

Only to my sub-cerebral surprise
at last on blasé sorrow
dawns an iota of disgust
for life's intemperance — — —

"As once you were"
with-hold your ghostly reference
to the sweet once were we— —

O leave me
my final illiteracy
of memory's languour

my preference
to drift in lenient coma
an older Ophelia
on Lethe

Hot Cross Bum

Beyond a hell-vermilion
curtain of neon
lies the Bowery

a lurid lane
leading misfortune's monsters

the human . . . race
altered to irrhythmic stagger

along the alcoholic's
exit to Ecstasia.

Impersonal as wind astray
confluent tides of swarm
loiter
in non-resistance calm
through dilatory
night and day

crowds of the choicelessly corrupted
disoriented

The Bowery sanctuary's
invasion by the vanquished
. . . in lazy anguish

Masquerade of Inexpressionism

inideate shutter
halting the bon-fire of the soul
from kindling the eyes

peep-holes of delight's observatory
stoppled by hinterland stupor
lunging a sullen blow on sunlight

indirective
abortive ocular
reception of the objective

Bum-bungling of actuality
exchanging
an inobvious real
for over-obvious irreal

faces of Inferno
peering from shock-absorbent
torsos

alternate with raffish saints'
eleemosynary innocence

Blowsy angels
lief to leer
upon crystal horizons

shelves of liquiescent 'beef'*
—staple fodder of their fanciful fall
a Brilliance all of bottles

*hard liquor

pouring a benison
of internal rain
leaving a rainbow in your brain

Hoary rovers
ignoring all but despicable directions,
shift through intentional trend of busymen

Their sailing, flailing limbs
of disequilibrium

clutching at wobbly banisters
to Elysium

Apart from them
a-sway the curb
one wry heckler
of an averse universe

spiring a querulous arm
announces the Tremendous

unto his vinous auditorium
of vast unfuture

A universe
to which (dead to the world)
he is ideologically deceased

graduate of indiscipline
post-graduate of procrastination

a prophet of Babble-on
shouts and mutters
to earless gutters

as inattentively
snobs of inertia
turning a dorsal retaliation
on closed entrance

block door-way stairs
with shoeless tiers
of Bandage-footed thins

lifting so daintily
the lusty lice
from their uncovered shins

At last
in a lucent grocery
the murmur of the mass
is become lingua audibly
in sodden-mouthed excuses

One lone lout
flecked with opal bruises
of belaboured bone
hurls an appeal-assault
on my comprehension

pinning my ear to his desperation
crying,
"It isn't my fault"

—A truth psychiatry
weighs courteously.

How idly
even
infinite dole

of pity
yearns your way

for none can enter
to the sot's account
one cent's worth
of Salvation
... that inborn fortune
self control

Despite that nowhere else
is Bumhood
handled with such gentleness

an onfall
of somewhat heavenly loaves
for your loafing
is the fashion

conditional compassion:
appreciation
of your publicity value
to the Bowery

So here comes help
here comes regeneration
—even a little alimentary fun
you shall not be left in the lurch

Some passing church
or social worker

confides to a brother
how he has managed to commandeer
a certain provision
of hot-cross buns

his earnestness
hushed by the hiccough holocaust
of otiose
hoboes hob-nobbing
with obtund oafs

in candid cupidity
and oathy psalmody

optimists conducting their poll
of the total calories in alcohol

or describing the sweet inward
upward of "creepy Pete"*

upward—
a flight into celestial resort

to alight in visceral discord

Sample interpolations of the Absolute
Physiognomy exhibiting

—the unseen pallor of a Negro
a Nordic's inner darkness

a silly smile immune to meaning
streaming the static transit of the street
to indecision's crossroads

where zest for zenith
zig-zag to zero
                    meet:

*wine

the egoless eagerness
of priestly patience
for laic participance

with
impious mystics of the other extreme
shrunken illuminati
sunken
rather than arisen

avid for infamous incense
of Bacchus' raucous breath

avoiding narrow breadth
of theology's
protect-drapery

not loathing
their ragged habitat
of indwelt rifts of clothing

divers failures
to fit personality
in envelopes of rigidity

So wonder why
defeat
by dignity of the majority
oft reveals
in close-up of inferno face
a nobler origin
than practicality's elite

Yet, if perchance
observed in down-sight from tall tower

lost it is
in grey dis-synthesis

of our adamic insects'
collision with confusion

Warfare in allure
of church and bar
oppositional altars
of cross and carousal
both irreconcilable
to well-faring flesh

As if should wish Evolution,
some esoteric union
of Mission and gin-mill
must breed eventually
someones more amenable
to ecstasy

than this unlikely spill
of God's mysteriously
variously
retarded children.

Nonetheless

Ardent self-crossing
kneeling-scaling
of steps inciting even the accursed
to church

proves unavailing
for visionary drunkard
inspired

to search intuitively desired
uni-identity

of primary
satieties of craving

Holy anomoly!

the gin-mill eased him out
the church now chucks him out.

The while
on high
disputing
the sheer beauty
Catholicism
once patroned
to entice humanity

a dull-dong bell
thuds out admonishment
to worship

atonic metal
detonation
tolling a drudgery
of exoteric
redemption

whose cadence
of illenience
transforms the cross bewailed
to flammable timber
for over-heating
Hades

waylaying for branding
indirigible bums
with the hot-cross
of ovenly buns.

Death is about to egress from the church

an undertaker's ebon aide
lurks in the portal-to-the-immortal

Saunters steep steps
to fling wide open the glass
doors of an obesely curtained hearse
prior to reception
of consecrated corpse

dross of the soul
gross of the soil

Concordantly
a ravenous truck
comes to a churning stand-still
before the pious facade;
hiding the invitatory conveyance
and carriages of florists' grievance.

Collecting refuse more profuse than man
the City's circulatory
sanitary apostles
a-leap to ash-cans
apply their profane ritual
to offal

Dust to dust

Even a putrescent Galaxy
could not be left where it lay
to disgust

Scrapped are remains
empty cans remain.

And always on the trodden street
—the communal cot—

embalmed in rum
under an unseen
baldachin of dream
blinking his inverted sky
of flagstone

prone
lies the body of the flop
where'er he drop.

One still savors
the favor of Eros

In this sore cemetery of the Comatose
here lies . . .

the belier
of disbelief
in this brief
bystander

Aptest attainer
to apex of Chimera

Inamorato
of incognito ignis fatuus

fatuitous
possessor of thoroughfare

O rare behaviour

a folly-wise scab of Metropolis
pounding with caressive jollity
a breastless slab

his cerebral fumes
assuming
arms' enlacement

decorously garbed
he's lovin'up the pavement

—interminable paramour
of horizontal stature
Venus-sans-vulva—

A vagabond in delirium
aping the rise and fall

of ocean
of inhalation
of coition.

An Aged Woman

The past has come apart
events are vagueing
the future is inexploitable

the present   pain.

Not even pain has that precision
with which it struck in youth-time

More like moth
eroding internal organs
hanging or falling down
in a spoiled closet

Does your mirror Bedevil you
or is the impossible
possible to senility
enabling the erstwhile agile
narrow silhouette of self
to hold in huge reserve
this excessive incognito
of a Bulbous stranger
only to be exorcised by death

Dilation has entirely eliminated
your long reality.

>   Mina Loy
>   July 12th
>   1984

Moreover, the Moon — — —

Face of the skies
preside
over our wonder.

Fluorescent
truant of heaven
draw us under.

Silver, circular corpse
your decease
infects us with unendurable ease,

touching nerve-terminals
to thermal icicles

Coercive as coma, frail as bloom
innuendoes of your inverse dawn
suffuse the self;
our every corpuscle become an elf.

V

EXCAVATIONS AND PRECISIONS

(PROSE 1914–1925)

Loy's grave marker in a woodland cemetery in Aspen, Colorado (designed by Herbert Bayer; Franz Berko photograph)

Aphorisms on Futurism

DIE in the Past
Live in the Future.

THE velocity of velocities arrives in starting.

IN pressing the material to derive its essence, matter becomes deformed.

AND form hurtling against itself is thrown beyond the synopsis of vision.

THE straight line and the circle are the parents of design, form the basis of art; there is no limit to their coherent variability.

LOVE the hideous in order to find the sublime core of it.

OPEN your arms to the dilapidated, to rehabilitate them.

YOU prefer to observe the past on which your eyes are already opened.

BUT the Future is only dark from outside.
Leap into it—and it EXPLODES with *Light*.

FORGET that you live in houses, that you may live in yourself—

FOR the smallest people live in the greatest houses.

BUT the smallest person, potentially, is as great as the Universe.

WHAT can you know of expansion, who limit yourselves to compromise?

HITHERTO the great man has achieved greatness by keeping the people small.

BUT in the Future, by inspiring the people to expand to their fullest capacity, the great man proportionately must be tremendous—a God.

LOVE of others is the appreciation of one's self.

MAY your egotism be so gigantic that you comprise mankind in your self-sympathy.

THE Future is limitless—the past a trail of insidious reactions.

LIFE is only limited by our prejudices. Destroy them, and you cease to be at the mercy of yourself.

TIME is the dispersion of intensiveness.

THE Futurist can live a thousand years in one poem.

HE can compress every æsthetic principle in one line.

THE mind is a magician bound by assimilations; let him loose and the smallest idea conceived in freedom will suffice to negate the wisdom of all forefathers.

LOOKING on the past you arrive at "Yes," but before you can act upon it you have already arrived at "NO."

THE Futurist must leap from affirmative to affirmative, ignoring intermittent negations—must spring from stepping-stone to stone of creative explorations; without slipping back into the turbid stream of accepted facts.

THERE are no excrescences on the absolute, to which man may pin his faith.

TODAY is the crisis in consciousness.

CONSCIOUSNESS cannot spontaneously accept or reject new forms, as offered by creative genius; it is the new form, for however great a period of time it may remain a mere irritant—that moulds consciousness to the necessary amplitude for holding it.

CONSCIOUSNESS has no climax.

LET the Universe flow into your consciousness, there is no limit to its capacity, nothing that it shall not re-create.

UNSCREW your capability of absorption and grasp the elements of Life—*Whole*.

MISERY is in the disintegration of Joy;
Intellect, of Intuition;
Acceptance, of Inspiration.

CEASE to build up your personality with the ejections of irrelevant minds.

NOT to be a cipher in your ambiente,
But to color your ambiente with your preferences.

NOT to accept experience at its face value.

BUT to readjust activity to the peculiarity of your own will.

THESE are the primary tentatives towards independence.

MAN is a slave only to his own mental lethargy.

YOU cannot restrict the mind's capacity.

THEREFORE you stand not only in abject servitude to your perceptive consciousness—

BUT also to the mechanical re-actions of the subconsciousness, that rubbish heap of race-tradition—

AND believing yourself free—your least conception is colored by the pigment of retrograde superstitions.

HERE are the fallow-lands of mental spatiality that Futurism will clear—

MAKING place for whatever you are brave enough, beautiful enough to draw out of the realized self.

TO your blushing we shout the obscenities, we scream the blasphemies, that you, being weak, whisper alone in the dark.

THEY are empty except of your shame.

AND so these sounds shall dissolve back to their innate senselessness.

THUS shall evolve the language of the Future.

THROUGH derision of Humanity as it appears—

TO arrive at respect for man as he shall be—

ACCEPT the tremendous truth of Futurism
Leaving all those
        —Knick-knacks.—

Feminist Manifesto

The feminist movement as at present instituted is

Inadequate

Women if you want to realise yourselves—you are on the eve of a devastating psychological upheaval—all your pet illusions must be unmasked—the lies of centuries have got to go— are you prepared for the **Wrench**—? There is no half-measure—NO scratching on the surface of the rubbish heap of tradition, will bring about **Reform**, the only method is

Absolute Demolition

Cease to place your confidence in economic legislation, vice-crusades & uniform education—you are glossing over

Reality.

Professional & commercial careers are opening up for you—

Is that all you want ?

And if you honestly desire to find your level without prejudice—be **Brave** & deny at the outset—that pathetic clap-trap war cry **Woman is the equal of man**—

She is **NOT!**   for

The man who lives a life in which his activities conform to a social code which is a protectorate of the feminine element— ——is no longer **masculine**

153

The women who adapt themselves to a theoretical valuation of their sex as a relative impersonality , are not yet Feminine

Leave off looking to men to find out what you are not —seek within yourselves to find out what you are

As conditions are at present constituted—you have the choice between Parasitism, & Prostitution —or Negation

Men & women are enemies, with the enmity of the exploited for the parasite, the parasite for the exploited—at present they are at the mercy of the advantage that each can take of the others sexual dependence—. The only point at which the interests of the sexes merge—is the sexual embrace.

The first illusion it is to your interest to demolish is the division of women into two classes the mistress, & the mother every well-balanced & developed woman knows that is not true, Nature has endowed the complete woman with a faculty for expressing herself through all her functions—there are no restrictions the woman who is so incompletely evolved as to be un-self-conscious in sex, will prove a restrictive influence on the temperamental expansion of the next generation; the woman who is a poor mistress will be an incompetent mother—an inferior mentality—& will enjoy an inadequate apprehension of Life .

To obtain results you must make sacrifices & the first & greatest sacrifice you have to make is of your "virtue"
The fictitious value of woman as identified with her physical purity—is too easy a stand-by—— rendering her lethargic in the acquisition of intrinsic merits of character by which she could obtain a concrete value— therefore, the first self-enforced law for the female sex, as a protection against the man made bogey of virtue—which is the principal instrument

of her subjection, would be the <u>unconditional</u> surgical <u>destruction</u> <u>of</u> <u>virginity</u> through-out the <u>female</u> population at puberty—.

The value of man is assessed entirely according to his use or interest to the community, the value of woman, depends entirely on <u>chance</u>, her success or insuccess in manoeuvering a man into taking the life-long responsibility of her—
The advantages of marriage are too ridiculously ample— compared to all other trades—for under modern conditions a woman can accept preposterously luxurious support from a man (with-out return of any sort—even offspring)—as a thank offering for her virginity
The woman who has not succeeded in striking that advantageous bargain—is prohibited from any but surreptitious re-action to Life-stimuli—& entirely <u>debarred</u> maternity.
Every woman has a right to maternity—
Every woman of superior intelligence should realize her race-responsibility, in producing children in adequate proportion to the unfit or degenerate members of her sex—

Each child of a superior woman should be the result of a definite period of psychic development in her life—& not necessarily of a possibly irksome & outworn continuance of an alliance—spontaneously adapted for vital creation in the beginning but not necessarily harmoniously balanced as the parties to it—follow their individual lines of personal evolution—
For the harmony of the race, each individual should be the expression of an easy & ample interpenetration of the male & female temperaments—free of stress
Woman must become more responsible for the child than man—
Women must destroy in themselves, the desire to be loved—

The feeling that it is a personal insult when a man transfers
his attentions from her to another woman
The desire for comfortable protection instead of an intelligent
curiosity & courage in meeting & resisting the pressure of life
sex or so called love must be reduced to its initial element,
honour, grief, sentimentality, pride & consequently jealousy
must be detached from it.
Woman for her happiness must retain her deceptive fragility of
appearance, combined with indomitable will, irreducible
courage, & abundant health the outcome of sound nerves—
Another great illusion that woman must use all her
introspective clear-sightedness & unbiassed bravery to
destroy—for the sake of her self respect is the impurity of sex
the realisation in defiance of superstition that there is nothing
impure in sex—except in the mental attitude to it—will
constitute an incalculable & wider social regeneration than it
is possible for our generation to imagine.

Modern Poetry

Poetry is prose bewitched, a music made of visual thoughts, the sound of an idea.

The new poetry of the English language has proceeded out of America. Of things American it attains the aristocratic situation of vitality. This unexpectedly realized valuation of American jazz and American poetry is endorsed by two publics; the one universal, the other infinitesimal in comparison.

And why has the collective spirit of the modern world, of which both are the reflection, recognized itself unanimously in the new music of unprecedented instruments, and so rarely in the new poetry of unprecedented verse? It is because the sound of music capturing our involuntary attention is so easy to get in touch with, while the silent sound of poetry requires our voluntary attention to obliterate the cold barrier of print with the whole "intelligence of our senses." And many of us who have no habit of reading not alone with the eye but also with the ear, have—especially at a superficial first reading—overlooked the beauty of it.

More than to read poetry we must listen to poetry. All reading is the evocation of speech; the difference in our approach, then, in reading a poem or a newspaper is that our attitude in reading a poem must be rather that of listening to and looking at a pictured song. Modern poetry, like music, has received a fresh impetus from contemporary life; they have both gained in precipitance of movement. The structure of all poetry is the movement that an active individuality makes in expressing itself. Poetic rhythm, of which we have all spoken so much, is the chart of a temperament.

The variety and felicity of these structural movements in modern verse has more than vindicated the rebellion against tradition. It will be found that one can recognize each of the modern poets' work by the gait of their mentality. Or rather that the formation of their verses is determined by the spontaneous tempo of their response to life. And if at first it appears irksome to adjust pleasure to unaccustomed meters, let us reflect in time that hexameters and alexandrines, before they became poetic laws, originated as the spontaneous structure of a poet's inspiration.

Imagine a tennis champion who became inspired to write poetry, would not his verse be likely to embody the rhythmic transit of skimming balls? Would not his meter depend on his way of life, would it not form itself, without having recourse to traditional, remembered, or accepted forms? This, then, is the secret of the new poetry. It is the direct response of the poet's mind to the modern world of varieties in which he finds himself. In each one we can discover his particular inheritance of that world's beauty.

Close as this relationship of poetry to music is, I think only once has the logical transition from verse to music, on which I had so often speculated, been made, and that by the American, Ezra Pound. To speak of the modern movement is to speak of him; the masterly impresario of modern poets, for without the discoveries he made with his poet's instinct for poetry, this modern movement would still be rather a nebula than the constellation it has become. Not only a famous poet, but a man of action, he gave the public the required push on to modern poetry at the psychological moment. Pound, the purveyor of geniuses to such journals as the "Little Review," on which he conferred immortality by procuring for its pages the manuscripts of Joyce's "Ulysses." Almost together with the publication of his magnificent Cantos, his music was played in Paris; it utters the communings of a poet's mind with itself making decisions on harmony.

It was inevitable that the renaissance of poetry should proceed out of America, where latterly a thousand languages have been born, and each one, for purposes of communication at least, English—English enriched and variegated with the grammatical structure and voice-inflection of many races, in novel alloy with the fundamental time-is-money idiom of the United States, discovered by the newspaper cartoonists.

This composite language is a very living language, it grows as you speak. For the true American appears to be ashamed to say anything in the way it has been said before. Every moment he ingeniously coins new words for old ideas, to keep good humor warm. And on the baser avenues of Manhattan every voice swings to the triple rhythm of its race, its citizenship and its personality.

Out of the welter of this unclassifiable speech, while professors of Harvard and Oxford labored to preserve "God's English," the muse of modern literature arose, and her tongue had been loosened in the melting-pot.

You may think it impossible to conjure up the relationship of expression between the high browest modern poets and an adolescent Slav who has speculated in a wholesale job-lot of mandarines and is trying to sell them in a retail market on First Avenue. But it lies simply in this: both have had to become adapted to a country where the mind has to put on its verbal clothes at terrific speed if it would speak in time; where no one will listen if you attack him twice with the same missile of argument. And, that the ear that has listened to the greatest number of sounds will have the most to choose from when it comes to self-expression, each has been liberally educated in the flexibility of phrases.

So in the American poet wherever he may wander, however he may engage himself with an older culture, there has occurred no Europeanization of his fundamental advantage, the acuter shock of the New World consciousness upon life. His is still poetry that has proceeded out of America.

The harvest from this recent fertiliser is the poetry of E. E. Cummings. Where other poets have failed for being too modern he is more modern still, and altogether successful; where others were entirely anti-human in their fear of sentimentality, he keeps that rich compassion that poets having for common things leads them to deck them [sic] with their own conception; for surely if there were a heaven it would be where this horrible ugliness of human life would arise self-consciously as that which the poet has made of it.

Cummings has united free verse and rhyme which so urgently

needed to be married. His rhymes are quite fresh—"radish-red" and "hazarded," and the freeness of his verse gives them a totally new metric relationship.

But fundamentally he is a great poet because his verse wells up abundantly from the foundations of his soul; a sonorous dynamo. And as I believe that the quality of genius must be largely unconscious, I can understand how Cummings can turn out such gabble when he is not being sublime. He is very often sublime.

In reading modern poetry one should beware of allowing mere technical eccentricities or grammatical disturbances to turn us from the main issue which is to get at the poem's reality. We should remember that this seeming strangeness is inevitable when any writer has come into an independent contact with nature: to each she must show herself in a new manner, for each has a different organic personality for perceiving her.

When the little controversies over what is permissible in art evaporate, we will always find that the seeming strangeness has disappeared with them in the larger aspect of the work which has the eternal quality that is common to all true art.

Out of the past most poets, after all, call to us with one or two perfect poems. And we have not complained of being too poor. You will find that the moderns have already done as much.

H. D., who is an interesting example of my claims for the American poet who engages with an older culture, has written at least two perfect poems: one about a swan.

Marianne Moore, whose writing so often amusingly suggests the soliloquies of a library clock, has written at least one perfect poem, "The Fish."

Lawrence Vail has written one perfect poem, the second "Cannibalistic Love Song," a snatch of primitive ideation with a rhythm as essential as daylight. Maxwell Bodenheim, I think, had one among his early work, and perfect also is a poem of Carlos Williams about the wind on a window-pane.

Williams brings me to a distinction that it is necessary to make in speaking of modern poets. Those I have spoken of are poets according to the old as well as the new reckoning; there are others who are poets only according to the new reckoning. They are headed by the doctor, Carlos Williams. Here is the poet whose expression derives from his life. He is a doctor. He loves bare facts. He is also a poet, he must recreate everything to suit himself. How can he reconcile these two selves?

Williams will make a poem of a bare fact—just show you something he noticed. The doctor wishes you to know just how uncompromisingly itself that fact is. But the poet would like you to realize all that it means to him, and he throws that bare fact onto paper in such a way that it becomes a part of Williams' own nature as well as the thing itself. That is the new rhythm.

Preceptors of Childhood

or The Nurses of Maraquita

I. Lilah

Lilah was pale, and Maraquita loved her. She read her "Peep of Day," a pretty book about a pretty man, that made her cry.

Maraquita's introduction to crying without being hurt for it.

Lilah and Maraquita understood each other perfectly.

They read "Peep of Day" all over again, and the sauce of the "Last Supper" tasted of tears.

And Lilah wore a brooch of pale pink coral rose-buds, cool to the fingers. . . .

One day Maraquita threw a domino through the window-pane, and was punished by Mamma.

And after the psychic concussion, she was still alive.

. . . And Lilah was still there—and once she had been governess in a jewish family in Hungary.

And in Hungary you buried medlars under trees and dug them up when they were rotten.

And a cavalry officer had galloped after the beautiful daughter of the family—and rode her down—because she was a jewess.

So the world grew bigger than it had been . . . and Maraquita wondered where the domino went to, and she felt lonely, like the pretty man on the wooden cross.

And Lilah had kind soft hands, but not very useful . . . and Maraquita was never going to set any store by useful things again.

Lilah one morning wasn't there any more . . . Maraquita wondered what it was about mornings, that made her wake up.

II. Queenie

She had large eyes.

Maraquita feeling affectionate called her Black-beetle.

And "Black-beetle," who hadn't lost all her fun yet, let her.

But after a few more months had happened to her, she would rather Maraquita called her "Queenie."

Maraquita supposed she wanted to be called that way, because she hoped Victoria would die.

She liked grand funerals.

But Victoria wouldn't die.

And nothing happened.

She was very clever at finding streets.

All the streets were the same—bare and buff.

Sometimes a richer house would have pillars painted a dull red.

The more streets they saw—the less they had to say.

"Next week will come Good Friday," said Maraquita at the corner of Blenheim Terrace.

And after an hour and a half—they got back to the corner of Blenheim Terrace.

And Queenie answered. "Yes, next week will come Good Friday."

III. Nicky

Nicky was the governess that Mamma loved.

She was very good.

Her breath was damp on the back of your neck over lessons, and the gold tassel on her watch chain tickled.

Nicky could sharpen pencils as fine as a needle.

And she drew narcissi with them, shading them till they shone.

Maraquita respected her for it.

This was the only respect from Maraquita she was ever going to get.

Her forehead was too high, and her square red fringe wouldn't flatten to it.

Her face was spotted with sunrust.

Her nose was flat, and pinkly turned up at the tip.

Her teeth were yellow.

Her eyelashes were white.

Her sleeves were too short, and red hairs grew among the freckles above her wrists.

Her ears were flannelly!

She wore a brown velvet waistcoat to a plaid dress with glass buttons that rucked on her virgin bosom.

She was very good.

She only made Maraquita feel very sick.

She prayed at leather chairs in the morning, in the morning room.

And Maraquita curdled with shame for conversing with something she couldn't see.

And the coal-heaver outside was quite likely to look in.

Nicky lived in fearful conspiracy with Mamma for two years.

Twenty-four months of unbearable biliousness.

Maraquita grew very thin.

They gave her porridge—with lumps in it.

Maraquita didn't want it.

They gave her cod-liver oil.

For was she not the child of parents who never stinted of buying anything that was all for the best for her?

And it was best to go to bed early.

Maraquita went to bed at 7 o'clock, and Nicky was so good.

She sat outside the bedroom door—forever—with an open Bible, under the gas jet—so that Maraquita shouldn't play.

Maraquita knew very well what should be done with Nicky.

Nicky, who was so blushfully buttoned up, should be quite undressed and thrown into a cage of Lions; she should be married to a lion—and have children with Lion's manes and Nicky's freckles.

Then again Maraquita felt the damp breath down the back of her neck—and the lions ROARED and their claws scratched.

*   *   *   *   *   *   *   *   *

And it was beter Maraquita should go to school in the country—she was getting very thin.

Auto-Facial-Construction

The face is our most potent symbol of personality.

The adolescent has facial contours in harmony with the conditions of his soul. Day by day the new interests and activities of modern life are prolonging the youth of our souls, and day by day, we are becoming more aware of the necessity for our faces to express that youthfulness, for the sake of psychic logic. Different systems of beauty culture have compromised with our inherent right, not only to "be ourselves" but to "look like ourselves", by producing a facial contour in middle age, which does duty as a "well preserved appearance". This preservation of partially distorted muscles, is, at best, merely a pleasing parody of youth. That subtle element of the ludicrous inherent in facial transformation by time, is the signpost of discouragement pointing along the path of the evolution of personality. For to what end is our experience of life, if deprived of a fitting aesthetic revelation in our faces? One distorted muscle causes a fundamental disharmony in self-expression, for no matter how well gowned or groomed men or women may be, how exquisitely the complexion is cared for, or how beautiful the expression of the eyes, if the original form of the face (intrinsic symbol of personality) has been effaced in muscular transformation, they have lost the power to communicate their true personalities to others and all expression of sentiment is veiled in pathos. Years of specialized interest in physiognomy as an artist, have brought me to an understanding of the human face, which has made it possible for me to find the basic principle of facial integrity, its conservation, and when necessary, reconstruction.

I will instruct men or women who are intelligent and for the briefest period, patient, to become masters of their facial destiny. I understand the skull with its muscular sheath, as a sphere whose superficies can be voluntarily energised. And the foundations of beauty as embedded in the three interconnected zones of energy encircling this sphere: the centres of control being at the base of the skull and highest point of the cranium. Control, through the identity of your conscious will, with these centres and zones, can be perfectly attained through my system, which does not include any form of cutaneous hygiene, (the care of the skin being left to the skin specialists) except in as far as the stimulus to circulation it induces, is of primary importance in the conservation of all the tissues. Through Auto-Facial-Construction the attachments of the muscles to the bones are revitalised, as also the gums, and the original facial contours are permanently preserved as a structure which can be relied upon without anxiety as to the ravages of time. A structure which complexion culture enhances in beauty, instead of attempting to disguise.

This means renascence for the society woman, the actor, the actress, the man of public career, for everybody who desires it. The initiation to this esoteric anatomical science is expensive, but economical in result; for it places at the disposal of individuals, a permanent principle for the independent conservation of beauty to which, once it is mastered, they have constant and natural resource.

APPENDICES

Loy, ca. 1920, Man Ray photograph
(Collection Roger L. Conover)

Editorial Guidelines and Considerations

One of the aims of this edition is to establish a text for an elusive body of work by this century's most significant critically unrecognized modern poet. *A* text, but not *the* text, for as the poet and her work came into sharper focus, the idealized goal with which I began seemed perpetually to recede. When I started this project, I imagined arriving at one set of principles by which all editorial questions could be resolved. I imagined producing a definitive text, revealing the poet's intention for the posthumous publication of her work. But for anyone who knows the Mina Loy file and the history of ambiguous and unstable features surrounding her publications, the idea of determining a definitive text is wishful at best.

This recognition in no way lessens the responsibility to produce a reliable text; in fact, it underscores the importance of doing so and argues for the adoption of conservative editorial procedures which do not further destabilize the texts. At the same time, it acknowledges the textual impurities already there and the risk of introducing further impurities even as we try to keep our controls clean.

Consider the first three sections of this volume. For nearly two-thirds of the thirty-four poems, no manuscripts or page proofs have yet been found. We have only the published record, and we have to concede the fallibility of that record, even as we find ourselves relying on it, exclusively in many cases, as the *sine qua non* of our text. Many of Mina Loy's poems appeared in magazines that were not proofread; many poems were never even typewritten, but sent in handwritten form to friends, who then typed them up and sent them off to editors. Her first book was typeset by compositors who could not read English, let alone distinguish errors from experiments. If its publisher could let it go to press with its title misspelled, what would the complete corrigenda look like? There is no manuscript. We will never know.

An image, then: invisible texts behind texts, lost spellings behind corrections, secret erasures behind revisions. No edition can do full justice to this archaeology. One can only clean up the site. I believe that Mina Loy understood something about the dubious nature of textual production and the anxiety of authorship well before Roland Barthes announced the death of the author and Michel Foucault evoked an authorless world. Loy conceptualized authorial erasure long before "theory" did:

unauthorized by the present
these letters are left authorless—
have lost all origin
. . . .
The hoarseness of the past
creaks
from erased leaves
covered with unwritten writing
since death's erasure
of the writer — —

—"Letters of the Unliving"

In the absence of authoritative texts for many poems and printer's copies of manuscripts for all the poems, not to mention the lack of collections published during Loy's career, editorial discretion was required in developing this text. I have tried to balance what I know of the poet and her habits with the conventions of textual practice and with other poets', editors', and critics' reading of dubious passages. I adopted certain principles, but I have applied them flexibly. Specific problems are resolved not by *a priori* rules but on their own terms. It is necessary, for example, to arbitrate spelling in local contexts, rather than assuming that Loy always spelled a particular word the same way. Imposing a dictionary's uniform standard on her polyglot handling of the English language would distort the surface of her work. And yet there are times when patent spelling errors require correction. Not only does she frequently employ foreign and archaic words as if they belong to colloquial English usage, but her English maximizes heterographic and orthographic opportunities to create puns.

The textual notes follow the order in which the poems appear in this book. Each poem has its own note, and each note is prefixed by an entry which provides the following information: title; date of composition, if known; authorized initial publication, if any; location of manuscript, if known; copy-text followed for this edition; emendations to the copy-text. Emendations are keyed by line to the poem. Some entries also offer definitions of obscure or archaic terminology.

In most cases, this note is followed by an Editor's Note. My attempt in writing these notes was not to provide bibliographic or biographical information that is widely known, nor to offer critical refractions on every poem, but rather to establish Loy's work within the literary and historical contexts in which she wrote. The notes are especially intended for those pursuing further studies on Loy. For that reason, I often make reference to Loy's own comments concerning a particular poem, and to the comments or work of other editors or critics. The notes often contain information on the circumstances of a poem's initial publication, editorial transmission, or critical reception. Many notes offer social, historical, or cultural background. Others contain speculative or anecdotal information. The notes are never intended to preempt the text, to provide complete annotations, or to be read alone, but rather to provide readers with ideas, contexts, and sources to explore on their own.

TITLES: The titles used in this edition are those that Loy or her editors used when her poems first appeared in magazines or books. For previously unpublished poems, the titles are those found on the latest manuscript versions.

DATES AND ORDER OF POEMS: Unless otherwise stated in the notes, all poems are arranged in the order of composition within each section. The texts in Section V and the appendices are independently dated. Sections I, III, and IV correspond roughly to early, middle, and late stages of the poet's career. When Loy dated a manuscript herself, this is stated. When the date of composition is conjectural, this is indicated by the abbreviation *ca.*, for *circa* (e.g., ca. 1927). Conjectural dates are reasonable surmises based on internal references or external evidence, such as correspondence. Where neither conjectural nor actual dating is possible, the date of composition is "unknown" and the poem is placed according to the date of its first publication.

SELECTION OF POEMS: This book contains all but ten poems published during Mina Loy's lifetime, or about two-thirds of the poems she wrote—a more complete view of her work than readers ever had when she was alive. This selection includes all the poems which received any serious critical attention, with one exception, and many which did not. The publisher's parameters for this edition made it impossible to include Loy's longest poem, "Anglo-Mongrels and the Rose." This mock-heroic autobiographical "epic" was first published serially between 1923 and 1925, and was collected for the first time in *The Last Lunar Baedeker* (1982). Jerome Rothenberg has referred to it as "one of the lost master-poems of the twentieth century." Jim Powell considers it "a *major* contribution to the 'High Modernist' effort to recapture social and social-psychological portraiture from the novel through the formal device of the poetic *sequence*." Yet this poem remains little recognized. It is probably the single most important missing feature in the landscape of the modernist long poem, and deserves consideration alongside such canonical works as *The Waste Land, Hugh Selwyn Mauberly, A, The Bridge, Paterson, Briggflatts, The Comedian as the Letter C*, the *Cantos*, and *The Maximus Poems*.

I am still not completely comfortable with its exclusion. But to have included "Anglo-Mongrels and the Rose" would have meant relinquishing half the poems presently included or sacrificing the notes; it would have transformed this edition from a generous selection into something altogether different: *Anglo-Mongrels and the Rose and Other Poems.* I considered excerpting some of its most arresting sections, such as "The Surprise," "Illumination," "Contraction," and "Religious Introduction." But this would have meant trading in the architecture for a few bricks. I decided instead to seek separate publication of the entire text.

BASIS OF TEXTS: The texts in this edition come primarily from three sources: the periodicals in which they first appeared; Mina Loy's first book, *Lunar Baedeker* (1923); and the manuscripts preserved in the Collection of American Literature at the Beinecke Rare Book and Manuscript Library, Yale University. The notes indicate which source I have chosen as the copy-text for each poem. Because neither manuscripts nor printer's copies exist for so many indispensable texts that Loy or her agents committed to publication, both in magazine and book form, I have followed first published appearances in the case of almost all texts published during Loy's lifetime. In the cases of poems published posthumously or appearing here for the first time, I have gone back to the manuscript sources.

I include a number of texts which first appeared in periodicals for which manuscript texts do exist. While I have occasionally (e.g., "Parturition") waived the printed text in favor of manuscript readings, I do so only if there is evidence of editorial mishandling, authorial preference, or authorial objection to a local word, punctuation, or line. Such changes are recorded as emendations in the notes.

All poems which appeared first in *Lunar Baedeker* (1923) are included in this edition, and their publication in that volume is noted. But they serve as copy-texts only if their appearance in *Lunar Baedeker* also marked their first print appearance. Some poems included in this edition are at variance with the versions printed in *Lunar Baedeker and Time Tables* (1958) and *The Last Lunar Baedeker* (1982). The texts of the present edition are the preferred ones in all such instances.

No reader in the 1990s can experience these poems as Loy's contemporaries did when they first encountered her bold dashes crackling like Morse code across the pages of little magazines in the years before World War I. Then they were shocking examples of a new species of verse written in the spirit of a new literary ethos. Now they are part of the historical free-verse movement. But we can come closer to imagining that sensation if we read the same texts. So even if we cannot say with certainty, given the archival gaps, that these are the poet's final versions of her texts, their authenticity is established by virtue of being the texts which gave the public its first vision of Loy.

EMENDATIONS, SPELLING, AND MECHANICS: All editorial changes apart from inconsequential typographical usage deriving from an original publication's house style (such as final periods in titles or ornamental devices between stanzas) have been recorded as emendations in the notes. Unless it is apparent that inconsistencies in spelling, punctuation, or capitalization derive from oversight or unauthorized editorial intervention, I have let the poet's preferences stand. Emendations are described in the notes or simply listed. In such cases, the symbol] separates the emendation (left of]) from the replaced text (right of]), usually the first published version.

Loy left England at seventeen and never resumed her formal education. In a series of revealing letters written to her son-in-law, Julien Levy, in the 1930s, she referred to her lack of grammatical training as both a limitation and a defining advantage of her style: "I don't know what a participle is for instance—how can I find out? . . . Having no knowledge of rules to go by—I feel there's something wrong—& at the same time something right—I can't see it yet from the other side—the reader's side." By that time she was a competent speaker of English, French, German, and Italian, and could get by in Spanish. She described herself as thinking in "a subconscious muddle of foreign languages" and confessed to having "no notion of what pure English is—although I am intensely aiming at pure language." British, American, French, German, Italian, and Latin spellings, names, and usages mingle throughout her work, often in the same stanza.

"Colorless" and "odour" appear five lines apart in "Songs to Joannes," where "coloured" also appears. Elsewhere in that poem, "Forever" and "for ever" occur within the same stanza. These are but a few examples of the many inconsistent spellings I have let stand; I consider them not so much irregularities as essential voiceprints of her citizenship in the planet Language, or, as she described them, vestiges of her "anglo-mongrel" heritage.

Just as she drew upon foreign words, she also favored uncommon words and spellings, loan words, macaronic spellings, etonyms, and slang. It is impossible to read her without a dictionary, or to come away from her poems without wondering where she encountered some of the exotic curios in her lexical cabinet. Words like glumes, benison, baldachin, scholiums, ilix, slaked, froward, gravid, phthisis, cymophanous, sialagogues, agamogenesis, filliping, Peris. Her poetic vocabulary contains many words not found in modern dictionaries; others can be found there, but are designated as archaic, "rare." Likewise, her spellings are often archaic or have a pseudo-archaic ring: exstacy, quotidienly, frescoe, viscuous, shew, changeant, minnikin, vengence, carrousel.

Loy once told Levy that she had a "subconscious obsession that [she] was being dishonest if [she] ever used a combination of words that had been used before." She continued: "I was trying to make a foreign language—Because English had already been used by *some* other people." In the same letter (n.d., 1934?) she explained her "fear of the inner censor condemning me if I ever used the word that *is* in use." Throughout her career she made deft use of good words that were out of use, and when she couldn't find the word she needed, she created one. Many of her coinages are puns, often used in service of satire: peninsular, bewilderness. Some are of onomatopoetic origin: blurr. Others are nonce words enhancing syllabic occasions, slight variations of recognizable forms or Anglo-French constructions: loquent, exhilarance, pendulence, adjacence. They all stand. Following the copy-texts, I have also allowed nonstandard hyphenation to remain, whenever it is of possible visual or linguistic consequence: to-gether, over-growth.

Finally, I have tried to reproduce the graphic effects of blank spaces, dashes, indentations and inflected capitalizations as found in Loy's publications and manuscripts. Some holograph sources bear indeterminate cursive flicks which do not always have typographic equivalents. The transition from holograph to type or from one house style to another tends to destroy evidence of this sort, and forces the appearance of blank space, the character of letters, and the thickness of dashes to conform to the availability of fonts and the exigencies of a publisher's or printer's typographic methods or in-house conventions. The dash—one of Loy's preferred marks of punctuation—is imprecise and variable in cursive form. In this edition, dashes are generally expressed as em-dashes, unless it is clear that another mark was intended. More details of this nature are reported in Marisa Januzzi's dissertation, *Reconstru[ing] Scar[s]: Mina Loy and the Matter of Modernist Poetics* (Columbia University, forthcoming).

Notes on the Text

The following abbreviations are used in the Notes:

AC	Arthur Cravan
AK	Alfred Kreymborg
AS	Alfred Stieglitz
ASP	Alfred Stieglitz Papers, Beinecke Rare Book and Manuscript Library, Yale University
CB	Constantin Brancusi
CU	Rare Book and Manuscript Library, Columbia University
CVV	Carl Van Vechten
CVVP	Carl Van Vechten Papers, Beinecke Rare Book and Manuscript Library, Yale University
ENC	Naumburg Collection [Edward Naumburg, Jr.], Rare Books and Special Collections Library, Princeton University
EP	Ezra Pound
FMF	Ford Madox Ford [Ford Madox Hueffer]
FTM	Filippo Tomasso Marinetti
GN	Gilbert Neiman's letters to Mina Loy. Private Collection
GP	Giovanni Papini
GS	Gertrude Stein
HV	Holograph version (the letters HV denote that a holograph version of the text exists in the named collection or archive)
JCP	Joseph Cornell Papers, Archives of American Art, Smithsonian Institution
JL	Julien Levy's letters to Mina Loy. Private Collection
LB	*Lunar Baedeker* (Paris: Contact Publishing Co., 1923)
LBT	*Lunar Baedeker & Time-Tables* (Highlands, N.C.: Jonathan Williams, 1958)
*LLB*82	*The Last Lunar Baedeker* (Highlands, N.C.: Jargon Society, 1982; Manchester, England: Carcanet Press, 1985)
*LLB*96	*The Lost Lunar Baedeker* (New York: Farrar Straus Giroux, 1996)
MDL	Mabel Dodge Luhan
MDLP	Mabel Dodge Luhan Papers, Beinecke Rare Book and Manuscript Library, Yale University
ML	Mina Loy
MLL	Mina Loy's letters to Julien and Joella Levy. Private Collection
MM	Marianne Moore
MS(S)	Manuscript(s)
NC	Nancy Cunard
NCB	Natalie Clifford Barney

NOMS	Whenever these letters appear, they denote the fact that no manuscript, typescript, holograph version, galley, or proof has been found in any archive to date. A note carrying this symbol indicates that the poem or work to which it corresponds is based on the first published version.
RM	Robert McAlmon
SH	Stephen Haweis
TSE	Thomas Stearns Eliot
WAA	Walter Conrad Arensberg Archives, Francis Bacon Library
WCW	William Carlos Williams
WL	Wyndham Lewis Collection, Rare Book and Manuscript Collection [Carl A. Kroch Library], Cornell University
YCAL	Yale Collection of American Literature, Beinecke Rare Book and Manuscript Library, Yale University, Mina Loy Archive
YW	Yvor Winters

I. Futurism x Feminism: The Circle Squared
(Poems 1914 –1920)

1. Untitled poem, 1914 ("There is No Life or Death"). First published in *Camera Work* 46 (April [October] 1914, p.18). The signed, dated HV in ASP is divided into four 4-line stanzas and lacks punctuation except for dashes (after ll. 9–14) and a final period (after l. 16). The text of the present edition follows the poem's first publication.

Editor's Note: Shortly after MDL offered this poem to AS, editor of *Camera Work*, he accepted it. This acceptance should have resulted in ML's first published poem, but the issue of *CW* in which it was scheduled to appear was delayed by six months, allowing another poem, "Café du Néant" (n. 4), to appear first. ML's "Aphorisms on Futurism" (n. 51) had appeared in an earlier issue of *CW*, marking ML's first publication in any genre.

2. PARTURITION, 1914. First published in *The Trend* 8:1 (October 1914, pp. 93–94). A signed, dated HV in CVVP is identical to the first published version in substantives but varies from it in details of punctuation and spacing. In an otherwise friendly letter to her friend (*Trend* editor) CVV dated "2–13–1915—Firenze" (YCAL), ML explicitly objected to the punctuation that had been added in the printed version. The present text therefore follows the HV, with the exception of two ampersands (ll. 62, 63), which I have spelled out. Reprinted in LB without the final three lines.

Editor's Note: This poem, rather than the act of childbirth itself, was probably the subject of a comment ML made to CVV in a letter dated October 29, 1914 (CVVP): "I am glad to introduce my sex to the inner meaning of childbirth.

The last illusion about my poor mis-created sex is gone. I am sad." Mina Loy gave birth to her first child in 1904, a full decade before she wrote this poem. She also had children in 1907, 1909, and 1919.

As the putative first poem ever written about the physical experience of childbirth from the parturient woman's point of view, and the first poem in English to use collage as a texturing device, "Parturition" is a significant event in the history of modern poetry as well as the literature of modern sexuality. Virginia M. Kouidis was the first critic to observe this. Her monograph, *Mina Loy: American Modernist Poet* (Baton Rouge: Louisiana State University Press, 1980) was the first book-length study of ML. ML's biographer, Carolyn Burke, also offers a brief but useful discussion of this poem in her essay "The New Poetry and the New Woman: Mina Loy" (Diane Middlebrook and Marilyn Yalom, eds., *Coming to Light: American Woman Poets of the Twentieth Century* [Ann Arbor: University of Michigan Press, 1985], pp. 37–57).

3. ITALIAN PICTURES, ca. summer 1914. NOMS. First published in *The Trend* 8:2 (November 1914), pp. 220–22. This text follows the first publication, with one emendation. In "Costa Magic," Cesira suffers from "pthisis," emended here to "phthisis" (ll. 28, 51), an archaic term for tuberculosis and other wasting illnesses. Reprinted in *LB* as "Three Italian Pictures," with slight modifications, the most significant of which is a stanza break in "Costa Magic" between lines 21 and 22.

Editor's Note: ML spent the summer of 1914 recovering from a nervous breakdown, psychological illness, or depression of some kind in the Apennine mountain village of Vallombrosa, province of Florence, with MDL and her guests. CVV, the new editor of *Trend*, was among MDL's American visitors. At the same time, ML was having an affair with FTM (see n. 4) and preparing to extricate herself from her marriage to SH (1877–1969). ML spent much of the summer anxiously monitoring reports of the German invasion. Only in the fall of 1914 would ML return to 54, Costa San Giorgio, her hilltop residence in Florence (ca. 1907–16).

In *Sacred and Profane Memories* (London: Cassell and Company, n.d. [1932], p. 116), CVV recalls a conversation with ML at MDL's villa in Vallombrosa in August 1914. Leo Stein had been describing the Futurists' positions as a form of political protest, insisting that FTM glorified war and the machine aesthetic but understood little of music or painting. ML, according to CVV, "gave her sanction to this opinion, adding that the futurists also were violent against women and were determined eventually to bear their own children." ML then asserted that Italian women existed "only for one purpose." CVV and ML tried to make a list of Italian women who had made significant contributions outside of the arena of opera. This exercise led CVV to conclude that "Italian women do not appear to have left a deep impression on history."

Under CVV's editorship, *Trend* was committed to giving "the younger men free rein to experiment with new forms." *Trend* was the self-described enemy of "stupidity, banality, cant, clap-trap morality, Robert W. Chambersism, sensationalism for its own sake." But it soon lost its financial backing, if not its disingenuous editorial mission; after three issues under CVV, the magazine folded. Before doing so it had managed to introduce ML, "a painter of international fame . . . who is in sympathy with the Italian school of Futurists." It remains one of the most elusive of the many elusive magazines in which ML was published, escaping even Hoffman, Allen, and Ulrich's notice in their generally comprehensive survey of little magazines of the (1891–1946) period, viz., *The Little Magazine: A History and Bibliography* (Princeton University Press, 1946).

4. THREE MOMENTS IN PARIS, 1914. This sequence first appeared as a triptych in *Rogue* 1:4 (May 1, 1915), pp.10–11, although "Café du Néant" had already been published out-of-suite in *International: A Review of Two Worlds* 8:8 (August 1914, p. 255). "Café du Néant" was therefore ML's first published poem. CVV introduced ML's work to both magazines. The *International* [formerly *Moods* magazine] version of "Café du Néant" differs substantially from the only known MS (HV at CVVP), while the *Rogue* version does not. Therefore I have chosen the latter as my copy-text.

Rogue's double-column format restricted line lengths, causing many lines to run over; the lineation here preserves the lineation of the HV. I have made three emendations to the *Rogue* text, all in "Magasins du Louvre." Left of the emblem] is the text as presented here; right of the] is the corresponding text as published in *Rogue*. Line numbers correspond to the lineation of the present edition:

20: camellia] camelia
21: iridescent] irridescent
35: Having surprised] Having surprising

"One O'clock at Night" was omitted from *LB*; the other two sections ran as separate poems. One notable variation occurs in the *LB* version of "Café du Néant":

1: leaning   lighted] lighted   leaning (*LB*)

Editor's Note: "Three Moments in Paris" is the first of a series of poetic satires on gender roles and male/female relations which make up the bulk, but not all, of this section. Here, ML warms up her satiric voice to address some of the themes she explored during and immediately after the years she spent in Florence—male posturing, female dependency, marital appearance, sexual repression, romantic love. Here, too, she appropriates Futurist vocabulary in mocking defiance of Futurism's male constabulary. Informing these satires is her brief but imprinting affair with FTM (1876–1944), Futurism's founding impresario and chief ideologue, to whom "One O'clock at Night" is addressed. For the reader unfamiliar with ML, FTM, or Futurism's significance as a prototype for the historical avant-garde, some further background is necessary.

FTM's charismatic personality and graphic, grammatical, and lexical theories exerted a strong influence on ML long after their uncoupling. His manifestos calling for the revisualization of language, the abolishment of punctuation, and the liberation of words from conventional syntax appealed to ML's already experimentally inclined temperament. His proposed substitution of traditional sentence structure with the "bizarre rhythms of free imagination" struck her as challenging and logical—a revolutionary formula for a revolutionary age. And his summons to oppose the old poetry of nostalgic obligation with a new poetry of intellectual expectation seemed to beckon and encourage her own imagination.

Given her troubled marriage and her interest in the language-actions of Marinettism, it is difficult to determine how much of ML's initial flirtation with Futurism had to do with her personal infatuation with FTM, how much with the war propaganda that was sweeping Florence at the time, and how much with curiosity and rebellion. FTM was surrounded by the most intellectual and artistic men in Florence, people who shared an elective affinity for literature and the arts. As Italy was preparing to enter World War I, most of the poets, artists, musicians, and actors in Marinetti's circle were signing up. FTM himself volunteered in a cyclist unit. Futurists Umberto Boccioni (sculptor), Luigi Russolo (composer), and Antonio Sant'Elia (architect) likewise enlisted. ML would soon volunteer as a nurse in a Red Cross Hospital. And while it is doubtful that the thirty-two-year-old English poet would have agreed with the thirty-eight-year-old Italian polemicist's characterization of war as "the world's only hygiene," she fully embraced his enthusiasm for war and his antipathy toward pacifism. Describing "the effect a pacifist *young* man has on one here now" is impossible, she wrote CVV. "It almost amounts to the physical repulsion some people have for the sexually perverse." In other letters written to CVV and MDL during this period, she expressed her envy of young male soldiers going to the front, her desire for "some sort of military training [for] the women who want it," and her sensation of war as an aphrodisiac. "I've got the war fever so badly," she wrote to CVV in one letter. "My masculine side longs for war," she confessed in another (CVVP). In "Psycho-Democracy" (1920/*LLB*82), ML would later express a more favorable view of pacifism and renounce her views of militarism.

But that was later. FTM was a magnetic force for many who came into contact with his virile intellect and personality. For ML, it went even beyond that. His energy reignited her creativity and incited her dormant animus. He jump-started her out of depression into a period of intense productivity, as she explained to MDL unapologetically. In fact, she suspected that she was "the only female who has reacted to it [FTM's energy]—exactly the way . . . men do. Of course being the most female thing extant—I'm somewhat masculine" (MDLP).

To MDL again: "I am so interested to find I am a sort of pseudo-Futurist" (1914). But in other letters written at the height of her involvement with FTM, she adopted a more guarded stance. To her estranged husband, SH, she wrote: "Do not fear—I am not intellectual enough to have become a Futurist—but have given up everything else." And in still other letters to MDL she hedged her convictions: "I am in the throes of conversion to Futurism—but I shall never convince myself."

ML finally objected to FTM's promotion of misogyny. But did she also thrive under the male caste system over which he presided as patriarch? According to FTM, women embodied the *amore* to which the male gaze was susceptible, luring them away from the technological vision to which they should be devoting their full concentration. Sentiment, lust, and passion were weaknesses in men, brought on by the animal presence of women. While publicly defending the rights of suffragists, FTM found their eagerness for the right to vote "ridiculous," for "woman finds herself wholly inferior in respect to character and intelligence and can therefore be only a mediocre legislative instrument." Although he denied that these principles applied to individual women of ML's advanced nature, FTM publicly compared women to animals—"wholly without usefulness"—subbeings.

His misogynism was more editorially than behaviorally conspicuous. The ninth tenet of *The Founding and Manifesto of Futurism* (1909) declared "contempt for women" as one of the movement's sacred principles. The tenth tenet named "feminism" as one of the enemies Futurism would destroy. Although ML was assured by FTM that these were general principles, that she was a special case, this was a slap in the face of an entire gender—and she took offense at this attempt to extort the female race. In "Lions' Jaws" (n. 14), ML frames Marinetti's attempt to wheedle his way into the " 'excepted' woman's heart" in terms of moral choices and gender loyalties.

Like all of ML's affairs, this one ended abruptly. But she was quick to admit that the relationship had also had its benefits and was relatively sanguine about the loss. Soon she was writing to MDL that although FTM's "interest in me lasted only two months of war fever . . . I am indebted to [FTM] for twenty years added to my life from mere contact with his exuberant personality." In the same letter, she refers to her "utter defeat in the sex war," a sense of surrender that is alluded to again in "Lions' Jaws," qualified by a sense of having won a larger cause. Almost nonchalantly she asked MDL what she was "making of Feminism. I heard you were interested. Have you got any idea in what direction the sex must be shoved?" And to CVV she matter-of-factly mentioned a similar shift in focus: "What I feel now are feminine politics." While her poems would soon take stern measure of FTM and his sexist gang, her letters speak more about renewal and purpose than rejection and disillusion. In fact, she describes her sense of optimism about the future as an optimism borne of Futurism, and describes FTM not as a devil but as a fallen angel, "sent from heaven to put the finishing touch—& they say he is a brute to women!" (CVVP).

5. SKETCH OF A MAN ON A PLATFORM, ca. autumn 1914. NOMS. First published in *Rogue* 1:2 (April 1, 1915, p. 12). This text follows the *Rogue* text. Reprinted in *LB*, with no substantive changes.
Editor's Note: This is the first of five poems and two plays ML published in Louise [Mrs. Edgard Varèse] and Allen Norton's spirited Greenwich Village magazine, which advertised itself as "the Cigarette of Literature," and was affectionately referred to as "a necessary evil." Futurist rhetoric is satirically evoked throughout the poem. The pseudo-man on the platform flexing his male fallacies with untroubled superiority bears all the signs of a mock Marinetti. ML pulls the strings; Marinetti is reduced to an amusing spectacle—Marinetti as marionette.

6. VIRGINS PLUS CURTAINS MINUS DOTS, December 1914. First published in *Rogue* 2:1 (August 15, 1915, p. 10). The present text follows the *Rogue* copy text except for one variant, following the signed and dated (December 3, 1914) HV (CVVP). Stanza breaks in *Rogue* vary slightly from the HV.
    2: door's] doors
Editor's Note: The word "dot" (l. 5), from the Latin *dotem*, dowry, was followed by an asterisk and explanatory footnote in *Rogue*. The HV bears a similar annotation; thus the asterisk/footnote in the present version is an authorial gloss.

7. BABIES IN HOSPITAL, May 1915. First published in *Rogue* 2:2 [*n.s.*, 3:2] (November 1916, p. 6). This text follows the first publication except for the correction of a misspelling in l. 45 (irresistibly] irresistably). Two HVs of this poem (CVVP) indicate a possible stanza break at ll. 45/46.
Editor's Note: ML volunteered in a surgical hospital in Florence during World War I; she described the experience to CVV in a letter dated February 13, 1915 (CVVP):
In Italy they will cut through 2 inches wide and deep of a man's back while he is awake. O dear Carlo men stand pain so much better than women ever so much better. . . . I'm so wildly happy among the blood & mess for a change. . . . I stink of iodoform—& all my nails are cut off for operations—& my hands have been washed in iodine—& isn't this all a change?. . . . I will write a poem about it— & you should hear what a tramp calls Madonna when he's having his abdomen cut open without anaesthetic.

In another letter sent to CVV during this period, she made reference to this poem: "I enclose some slight things I thought about some babies I saw in a hospital. Florence is full of soldiers."

ML is listed among the November 1916 contributors to *Rogue* as "the writer, and Artist Englishwoman [who] has arrived in New York from Florence. Her first drawing done in this country is in this *Rogue*." The drawing, *Consider Your Grandmother's Stays*, occupied the page facing her poem and was the first of several she would publish in American periodicals.

8. GIOVANNI FRANCHI, ca. May–July 1915. First published in *Rogue* 2:1 [*n.s.* 3:2] (October 1916, p. 4). A single HV of this poem survives in CVVP, signed and dated "Mina Loy Forte-dei-Marmi 23 July 1915." This text follows the first published version, which differs from the HV only in accidentals. The emendations I have made to the *Rogue* text are left of the].

24–25: démodé] demode'
43: cymophanous] symophonous
48: filliping] fillipping
53, 115: Paszkowski's] Paschkowski's
(Paszkowski's was and still is a café-bar located on the north side of Piazza Vittorio Emanuelle, Florence; it was a gathering place for artists and intellectuals during ML's Florence years, as was the more famous Caffè Giubbe. ML frequented both. I thank Carolyn Burke and Marisa Januzzi for this information.)
136: mean] means
154: minarets] minarettes
155: mayonnaise] mayonaise

Editor's Note: The "Giovanni Bapini" of this satiric work is based on GP (1881–1966), one of ML's significant lovers and one of Futurism's philosophical fathers, caricatured more as foolosopher here. Papini began his career as an "anti-philosopher." His first book, *Twilight of the Philosophers* (1906), was one of the foundation texts for FTM's Futurism, just as *Lacerba*, the journal he founded in 1913, was an important outlet for FTM's polemical writing. Despite the appearance of solidarity, the two were uneasy colleagues; the charismatic and worldly FTM and the socially insecure and visually impaired GP formed a convenient intellectual alliance that belied a deep personal distrust and competition. This was not helped by GP's discovery that ML was taking turns with both of them in bed. The exposure of this love triangle put a wedge in the fragile geometry of all three familiars and hastened ML's divorce and first trip to America. It also exposed the gap between FTM's practice and teachings, for the "adulterous triangle" was supposedly one of the "four intellectual poisons" that he wanted to abolish (*War, the World's Only Hygiene*).

In a letter to CVV written shortly after the triangle broke up, ML rationalized her behavior: "Of course I was in the right having acted entirely in the wrong." After losing FTM, she was not regretting the past as much as she was dreading the future: "The only thing that troubles me is the fear of not finding someone who appeals to me as much" (CVVP).

The split in Futurist ranks that followed was explained in terms of philosophical differences but was grounded in sexual politics. GP won a number of the movement's younger disciples to his side, and the biographically unidentified "Giovanni Franchi" of this poem is probably modeled after one of his junior admirers. In an undated letter to CVV, ML wrote of GP: "He's going to ruin himself—getting narrower & narrower—& when I try to wake him up—he says the medicine's too strong—decidedly New York I think—don't you?" Elsewhere she expressed a more disdainful view of GP: "Friends keep me posted as to the errors of his flesh. . . . He's really only a fool . . . & his imagination's gone to pot."

Still elsewhere, ML reports to CVV with a touch of sadistic pleasure the play of her ideas on GP's head: "I had a lovely argument with Papini—I maintained that pederasty was the highest and noblest form of love—& gave the most conclusive reasons—which he couldn't deny—but [he] ended up by saying it's morally and physically abhorrent. So you see?"

Describing her guests, MDL sometimes spoke endearingly of her "pederasts." Discussions on such topics as pederasty, perversion, adultery, pornography, free love, exhibitionism, and homosexuality were common among the reformers, iconoclasts, and artists who visited MDL's Villa Curonia and frequented Paszkowski's; the new thinkers enjoyed expressing their support for such behavior, although their persuasion was often more rhetorical than behavioral. Sex was the most intriguing conversational subject from which taboo and superstition had been lifted in the new permissive culture. And sex was the favorite subject at MDL's gatherings, where tolerance was encouraged and inhibition ridiculed. ML preferred this subject to all others and enjoyed taking extreme positions to challenge and goad her listeners.

CVV was the husband of Fania Marinoff, but did not make a secret of his occasional affairs with men. ML knew he would find the image she presented an amusing one: GP in the awkward spot of having to take a stand on sodomy after listening to his ex-lover extol the virtues of pederasty. The sexually challenged GP had been a jealous lover before she left him and still had not reconciled himself to the separation. He blamed FTM and was avenging his bruised heart by cultivating protégés in an effort to draw followers away from his rival's splintering movement. GP would not have been at all amused by having his sexual preference questioned, nor by ML's cynical depiction of the elder Giovanni's infatuation with the younger Giovanni in "Giovanni Franchi." It is hard to imagine a greater affront to Futurist sensibilities than the insinuation of homosexual attraction between the mentor and the mentored. The Futurists were steadfast in their masculine pose and saw no humor in their masquerade of manliness; they were hysterical in their defense of virility and even defended rape as the procreative prerogative of victors in war—life must be re-created out of death on the battlefield. ML's poem bites farcically into the pretense of pedantic male posture and twists with subversive wit the nature of Futurist homophilia.

On the surface, "Giovanni Franchi" is an entertaining lampoon of an apprentice philosopher learning the ways of the world at the feet of his pretentious and intellectually vain elder while three females of indiscrete identity patter complaisantly at the edges of male banter. The insidious subtext only emerges when the incriminating portrait of the Futurist as Pederast is in full view. At the same time, it is difficult not to imagine ML as the self-accusing speaker, reproaching herself for what she didn't see until too late—the true nature of the recused man. She alone "never knew what he was / Or how he was himself" (ll. 124/125). Now that she understands, she consoles herself. She could not have won, could not even have competed with the object of the elder philosopher's infatuation: a handsome boy in adolescence with "sensitive down among his freckles" (1.46). She acknowledges with irony and a hint of mock jealousy the qualities she lacked that Giovanni Franchi had, before reducing him to his only advantage. Indeed: "His adolescence was all there was of him" (l.11).

"He was so young / That explains so much" (ll. 77–78).

9. AT THE DOOR OF THE HOUSE, ca. 1915. NOMS. First published in *Others: An Anthology of the New Verse* (New York: Knopf, 1917), pp. 64–66. The present text follows the 1917 version, to which I have made two emendations:

    8: inconducive] incondusive
    46: aniline] analine

Editor's Note: MM, Wallace Stevens, WCW, and TSE also appeared in AK's second *Others* anthology. EP, in his famous review of this anthology in *The Little Review* 4:11 (March 1918, pp. 56–58), praises AK for "this first adequate presentation of ML and MM"; he takes their work to be a "distinctly national product" and praises AK for "getting his eye in." In this first attempt at literary classification of ML's work, EP coined the term "*logopoeia* or poetry that is akin to nothing but language, which is a dance of intelligence among words and ideas and modification of ideas and characters," as distinct from *melopoeia* ("poetry which moves by its music") or *imagism* ("poetry wherein the feelings of painting and sculpture are predominant").

However problematic certain aspects of Pound's characterization may appear in retrospect, this was the first significant critical notice of ML's poetry to appear in print, the first of many comparisons to MM, and the first to invoke the name of Jules Laforgue. More important, EP immediately recognized the cerebral nature of ML's work and predicted that it would be dismissed for its difficulty: "One wonders what the devil anyone will make of this sort of thing who hasn't all the clues. . . . I am aware that the poems before me would drive numerous not wholly unintelligent readers into a fury of rage-out-of-puzzlement." Two months later, TSE weighed in with his opinion of the *Others* anthology. Writing in *The Egoist* V (May 1918, p. 70) under the pseudonym T. S. Apteryx, Eliot praised Loy more reservedly: "It is impossible to tell whether there is a positive *oeuvre* or only a few successes." Although TSE never revisited that question, or commented on ML again, the aleatory foundation of this poem may have adumbrated the Tarot imagery in *The Waste Land* (1922).

Conrad Aiken also reviewed the *Others* anthology in his *Skepticisms: Notes on Contemporary Poetry* (New York: Knopf, 1919). He didn't think much of AK's enterprise and encouraged readers not to waste their time on the "gelatinous quiverings of Mina Loy."

10. THE EFFECTUAL MARRIAGE, *or* THE INSIPID NARRATIVE OF *GINA AND MIOVANNI*, ca. summer 1915. NOMS. First published in *Others: An Anthology of the New Verse*, pp. 66–70. The parenthetical postscript is reproduced here as it appeared in the first published version. ML spent the summer of 1915 in the Italian seaside resort of Forte dei Marmi. This version follows the first publication, to which I have made the following emendations:

5: Gina] Gian
23: correlative] correllative
60: idiosyncrasies] idiosyncracies
87: variegate] varigate

Editor's Note: "Gina" and "Miovanni" stand for ML and GP. This poem drew early and favorable comments from both EP and TSE, and has commanded as much critical attention as any poem from ML's Florence period. TSE pronounced it "extremely good, and suggestive of Le Bosschère." EP found it "perhaps better written than anything I have found in Miss Moore." Later, EP excerpted this poem in two anthologies, under the title "Ineffectual Marriage." In 1932 he still considered "The Effectual Marriage" one of the most memorable poems of the last thirty years, one which defined its epoch. But in memorializing the poem, he also distorted it. Burke has written persuasively about the effect of Pound's "framing" of this poem. See Burke's essays "Getting Spliced: Modernism and Sexual Difference" (*American Quarterly* 39 [1987, pp. 98–121]) and "Mina Loy," in Bonnie Scott, ed., *The Gender of Modernism* (Bloomington: Indiana University Press, 1990).

11. HUMAN CYLINDERS, ca. 1915. NOMS. First published in *Others: An Anthology of the New Verse*, pp. 71–72. This text follows the first published version, to which I have made one emendation:

33: antediluvian] antedeluvian

Editor's Note: For EP, the 1917 *Others* anthology contained the first "adequate presentation" of ML's work. For John Rodker (1894–1955), the three poems by ML also enabled one to "estimate her actual significance" for the first time. But he was less taken by the evidence than EP, concluding that "she certainly is a poet, but her work remains only—very interesting. Between that and poetry that matters is still a wide gulf. Her visualization is original, often brilliant, but headwork is cold comfort and her capacity for feeling is rather a cold indignation." He gave qualified praise to "Human Cylinders," calling it "a good poem," but suggesting that if only it were "simplified, it might be great" (*Little Review* 5:7 [November 1918, pp. 31–32]). The twenty-four-year-old reviewer probably knew very little, if anything, of the Futurist sources from which its lines were drawn. (John Rodker was the founder of Ovid Press, publisher of EP's *Hugh Selwyn Mauberly*, and first husband of the English novelist Mary Butts).

12. THE BLACK VIRGINITY, ca. 1915. NOMS. First published in *Others: A Magazine of the New Verse* 5:1 (December 1918, pp. 6–7). This text follows the first publication. I have made the following emendations to the 1918 text:

    10: Truncated] Troncated
    11: segregation] segration
    17: Anaemic] Aenaemic
    38: Subjugated] Subjuguted

13. IGNORAMUS, composed ca. 1915. NOMS. First published in *LB* (section 1: "1921–1922"). Although not published until 1923, ML refers to this poem in a letter to CVV written in 1915: "The best thing I did was 'Ignoramus' " (CVVP). Thus I have placed the composition date at 1915. This text follows the first publication, except for the following emendations:

    28: Mating] Making
    53: last"] last

Editor's Note: The title character of this poem is a purehearted and innnocent-natured tramp—very much in the spirit of Charlie Chaplin's tramp, who first made his screen appearance in the 1910s. This poem reveals a day in the tramp's life—a life of disadvantage, resourcefulness, routine, and chance. Performing, maundering, bargaining, improvising, playing, "breakfasting on rain"—these are among the survival habits and alleviating solutions of the sentient alley dwellers and outcasts on whom ML shined her final gaze of compassion—after abandoning society, satire, and homage. "Ignoramus" represents the first appearance of such a figure in ML's work, prefiguring the lowlife figures featured in several poems written during her Bowery period (Section 4).

14. LIONS' JAWS. Composition date unknown, ca. 1919. NOMS. "Lions' Jaws" appears to be ML's final verse verdict on Futurist affairs—her own, her paramours', their victims', their lovers'. First published in *The Little Review* 7: 3 (September–December 1920, pp. 39–43). The present text follows the first published version except for the following emendations:

    5: mise en scène] mis-en-scene
    24: rococo] rococco
    49: carnivorous] carniverous

53: lightning] lightening
76: on a] an a
81: vermilion] vermillion
89: ménage] menage

Editor's Note: This was the first of three contributions by ML to *The Little Review*, the influential magazine whose foreign editor, EP, solicited ML's poems. This issue of *LR* also contained a review by John Rodker of the latest *Others* anthology (*Others for 1919: An Anthology of the New Verse*) and a response by ML (see n. 17).

Previous notes have identified some, but not all, of the identities behind the spoof aliases of "Lions' Jaws." "Danriel Gabrunzio" is Gabriele D'Annunzio (1863–1938), Italian nationalist, poet, adventurer, and adulterer. "Raminetti" is of course FTM; "Bapini" is GP, the homely Futurist scholar and nearsighted philosopher introduced in "Giovanni Franchi" and "The Effectual Marriage." "Ram" and "Bap" are mock pet names for competitors Marinetti and Bapini, reminiscent of the sounds of boys playing with toy artillery. And they are both "flabbergasts," in other words, Futurists. "Imna Oly," "Nima Lyo," and "Anim Yol" all refer to ML, who sometimes used these acronymic aliases when referring to herself in the third person. "Imna Oly," incidentally, made another appearance in 1920. In a Provincetown Players playbill announcing Laurence Vail's *What d'You Want?* at the Selwyn Theater on Broadway (December–January, 1919–20), "Imna Oly" played the part of "Esther, a spinster." Finally, "Mrs. Krar Standing Hail" (l. 124) is a stand-up jab at Mrs. Stan Harding Krayl (a.k.a. Mrs. Gardner Hale), a friend of MDL who had an affair with ML's husband, SH, in Florence. This relationship is described in some detail in the "Stephen Haweis" chapter of MDL's autobiographical narrative, *Intimate Memories: European Encounters* (New York: Harcourt Brace and Company, 1935).

Compositionally this poem belongs with ML's post-Florence poems. Its attenuating opening line ("Peninsular" is allowed to stand as a pun) and telescopic perspective throughout place the personalities and events described on memory's horizon. ML was probably living in New York when she wrote this poem, but because "Lions' Jaws" is set in Italy and represents ML's last balance sheet of Futurist business, I am including it in this section. The poem could not have been written before 1919, since the last stanza makes reference to Gabriele d'Annunzio's famous storm on the contested Adriatic port of Fiume, which took place in September of that year. D'Annunzio's unauthorized siege was designed to prevent Fiume's incorporation into the then newly formed Yugoslav nation.

Much of the private and public history of ML and the Futurists can be traced in this poem, not to mention the personality traits, ideological tendencies, and character flaws of the protagonists, from FTM's fantasy of self-propagation ("agamogenesis"), to GP's sense of inferiority, to D'Annunzio's insatiable lust for military and sexual trophies. ML is finally capable, at this remove, of viewing her first battle in the sex war as both a personal defeat and a moral victory, and can concede that the complicity, if not duplicity, of her status as an "excepted" woman was a trap which left her with only one choice. I do not wish to transpose too much biography onto this poem, but there is also the suggestion that she may have fantasized—if not actually petitioned—her lovers to father (another) illegitimate child, just as there are hints elsewhere that she may have miscarried or aborted a child by SH.

It seems just to give ML the last word in this particular chapter of her literary struggles on the hom(m)e front:

"Now dear Carlo—If you like you can say that Marinetti influenced me—merely by waking me up—I am in no way *considered* a Futurist by futurists—& as for Papini he has in no way influenced——*my work*!! so don't say a word about it—he's very passatist—really" (ML to CVV, 1914; CVVP).

II. Songs to Joannes
(1917)

15. SONGS TO JOANNES. By early 1917 ML had completed this sequence. She had drafted most of it by August 1915, and made frequent references to the work-in-progress in letters she wrote to CVV that year. Initially, she expressed hesitation about the work (". . . no interest to the public . . . for your eyes only") and concern about circulating it at all: "I feel my family on top of me—they want to read some of my pretty poems!. . . . one friend . . . has dubbed my work pure pornography—". When SH warned her that she was ruining her reputation by writing as she did, she was annoyed and discouraged. But as the year and sequence matured, it was clear that the poem had introjected itself deeply within her psyche: "If this book of mine is no good it settles me—I am the book and I have that esoteric sensation of *creating*!" By the time she had completed the project, she could hardly contain her eagerness to make it public: "I send herewith—the second part of Songs to Joannes—*the* best since Sappho—they are interesting. . . . If you wanted me to be a happy woman for five minutes or more, you would get [them] published. . . . My book is wonderful—it frightens me."

In July 1915, the first four sections of what was eventually to become a thirty-four-song cycle appeared under the title "Love Songs" in the inaugural issue of *Others: A Magazine of the New Verse* (1:1, July 1915, pp. 6–8). The scandal created by the debut of *Others* quickly earned the magazine "a reputation bordering on infamy," AK recalled two decades later in *Troubadour: An Autobiography* (New York: Liveright, 1925). He proudly described the "small-sized riot" that broke out when *Others* first hit the stands. ML's "Love Songs" were the favorite victim of the attacks: "Detractors shuddered at Mina Loy's subject-matter and derided her elimination of punctuation marks and the audacious spacing of her lines," not to mention her explicit examination of intercourse, orgasm, bodily function, and sexual desire. Although she was yet to make her first trip to America, ML had already secured her reputation in the New York avant-garde literary community. In his famous survey of American poetry, *Our Singing Strength* (New York: Coward-McCann, 1929), AK again described the "violent sensation" that ML's "Love Songs" created: her "clinical frankness [and] sardonic conclusions, wedded to a madly elliptical style scornful of the regulation grammar, syntax and punctuation . . . drove our critics into furious despair. . . . The utter nonchalance in revealing the secrets of sex was denounced as nothing less than lewd. It took a strong digestive apparatus to read Mina Loy. . . . To reduce eroticism to the sty was an outrage, and to do so without verbs, sentence structure . . . [was] even more offensive." AK was referring to the sty of the limicolous "Pig Cupid" in ML's all-business opening stanza to "Love Songs," the most famous of all her lines.

In recalling the outrage of "the average critic . . . here in enlightened Manhattan" toward "Love Songs" in general and its first stanza in particular, AK also made reference to lineal qualities of another nature. He described the poet as the "exotic and beautiful . . . English Jewess, Mina Loy, an artist as well as a poet," then described her avant-garde credentials: "She imbibed the precepts of Apollinaire and Marinetti and became a Futurist with all the earnestness and irony of a woman possessed and obsessed with the sense of human experience and disillusion." AK was the first writer to explicitly acknowledge ML's debt to FTM's Futurist manifestos, or to comment directly on her syntax and subject matter in terms of Futurist technique. Her replacement of "the foolish pauses made by commas and periods" with the more intuitional blank spaces and dashes, her mixing of upper- and lower-case letters, her early use of collage and disjunction, and the charged sexual energy of her poems reflect the influence of FTM and are consistent with the principles he advocated in his manifesto "The Destruction of Syntax" (1913). That ML used these techniques in service of aims directly anathematical to FTM's makes the cultural impact of her appropriation all the more significant. When her lover became the "other," she turned his tools into her weapons.

"Had a man written these poems," AK recalled of "Love Songs," they might have been tolerated. "But a woman wrote them, a woman who dressed like a lady and painted charming lamp-shades." Her title promised romance. But her songs delivered unmelodic sex. *Chansons sans chanson.*

AK's comment was the first to acknowledge a deeply gendered, largely unspoken bias on the part of the critical establishment's initial reaction to these transgressive lyrics. AK recalled that the early reviews of "Love Songs" puzzled ML as much as they injured her. This was also true of the early rejections, which ML referred to in a letter addressed to CVV (n.d., 1915). CVV had been encouraging her to write "something without a sexual undercurrent." Her response: "I know nothing but life—and that is generally reducible to sex. . . .

Apro-po of Joannes Songs—why won't the pubs publish [?]. This is very sad.
And why did Amy Lowell *hate* my things? . . . Dear Carlo, I'm trying to think
of a subject that's not sexy to write about . . . & I can't in life."

By 1920, free love was the toast of free verse; E. E. Cummings and Edna St.
Vincent Millay were considered the ultra-sexual poets of the hour. ML's ex-
periments had helped clear a path for both, but she was already being trimmed
out of modern poetry's body as if she was a premature growth.

If critics reacted quickly to the publication of "Love Songs," ML did, too.
Within weeks, she wrote to CVV that she liked "the tendency of *'Others'* and
the way it look[ed but was] rather sorry that some words were misprinted such
as . . . 'Sitting the appraisable' [l. I.2] instead of silting the appraisable—and
'there are' instead of 'these are suspect places' [l. I.13]." Comparing the 1915
Others text to the only known MS of this poem (a signed and dated [1915] HV
of I–IV), it is evident that the errors she referred to were not present in the
handwritten text (CVVP). But it is also possible to see how the words in question
could be misread by less than astute surveyors of her casual cursive script.
Fragmentary drafts of other "Love Songs" exist at YCAL, but not in sufficiently
whole or finished states to serve as copy-texts.

Two years later the complete sequence appeared, taking up an entire issue
of *Others* (3:6, April 1917, pp. 3–20). The above-mentioned errors had been
corrected, but certain other changes inconsistent with the HV and the 1915
printing were introduced. Some of them clearly bore ML's signature. For ex-
ample, the last four lines of IV in 1915:

> *For I had guessed mine*
> *That if I should find YOU*
> *And bring you with me*
> *The brood would be swept clean out*

became two in 1917:

> *Before I guessed*
> *—Sweeping the brood clean out*

Other changes were more questionable (e.g., "white and star-topped" re-
placed "white star-topped" in l. I.6; "sewn" replaced "sown" in l. I.7; "spill't"
replaced "spilled" in l. III.5). ML had not indicated that these lines contained
errors in her 1915 complaint. More important, she reverted to the original HV
of lines I.6 and I.7 when she reformulated the sequence in 1923 (*LB*), seemingly
confirming her original textual intent.

But *LB* preserved other changes made in 1917, such as the ending of IV. At
this remove, in the absence of proofs bearing her corrections, it is impossible to
distinguish printer's errors from editorial changes from ML's own alterations or
to know what "repairs" she might have made in 1917, then reconsidered in
1923. My assumption, finally, is that the 1917 rendering of l. I. 6–7 is either
non-authorial or an authorial revision that was later recanted; that it does not
stand. The only evidence that I have ever found indicating that proofs of *LB* ex-

isted is RM's casual statement quoted in Robert E. Knoll, ed., *McAlmon and the Lost Generation* (Lincoln: University of Nebraska Press, 1962, p. 226), where he mentions checking proofs of *LB* in Rapallo, Italy, en route from Spain to France.

For the 1917 publication, ML made sure to correct the errors that bothered her most in 1915, substituting "silting" for "sitting" (l. I.2) and "These" for "There" (l. I.13) in the opening section. Beyond that, she made a few new revisions (e.g., the ending of IV) before publishing the sequence in *Others*. The surprising appearance of "sifting" (l. I.2) in *LB* in place of what had been wrongly printed as "sitting" (1915) and corrected to "silting" (HV, 1917) is a possible late revision, but more likely a printer's error. Or, as Januzzi has suggested, this could reflect ML's attempt to rectify what she knew had been a problematic line in 1915—having forgotten her earlier solution.

I do not view the *LB* rendition of "Love Songs" as an attempt to put the 1917 cycle into final order but rather as a separate narrative involving many of the same strategies. The result is an altogether different—and arguably less successful—effort. Therefore I present the *LB* version in Appendix D.

The text of "Songs to Joannes" presented here necessarily relies on the 1917 *Others* version as its copy-text, and varies from it in relatively few instances. The 1917 text, after all, is the source for thirty of the thirty-four original parts. I rely on ML's letters, and variants in the earlier (HV) and later (*LB*) versions, only to mediate discrepancies in I–IV, as mentioned above. In most instances, first and final intentions converge. Where they do not, the copy-text or editorial judgment prevails.

In the present edition, I have not prefaced this sequence with the dedicatory poem, "To You" (*Others* [July 1916, pp. 27–28]), as I did in *LLB*82. Januzzi has persuaded me that despite ML's plea to CVV [(n.d., 1915) to "get Songs for Joannes published for me—all together—printed on one side of each page only—& a large round in the middle of each page—& one whole entirely blank page with nothing on it between the first and second parts—(pause in between moods)—the dedication—'TO YOU' ")], I may have taken this request too literally in *LLB*82. I believe her caution is correct. I now find it difficult to read "To You" as a prelude to "Songs to Joannes," either thematically or structurally. It has therefore been left out of the present edition altogether.

I explain these issues in detail for several reasons. This is among the most frequently discussed, excerpted, and anthologized of ML's poems; "Love Songs" and its often forgotten predecessor, "Songs to Joannes," have a particularly complicated textual and editorial history; certain lines, especially in the opening section which I have just been discussing, have been the subject of more speculation and uncertainty than any other lines she produced. My decisions should be subject to question, but my reasons should not.

I have made the following emendations to the 1917 text, and refrained from making others, as explained below. Dashes here (— — — —) correspond to dashes in Loy's 1917 text, and are counted as lines of type when they occupy a complete line, for example XXX.5. This is important only for the purpose of cross-referencing lines with emendations below. The *LLB*96 version is to the left of the]. The 1917 *Others* version is to the right:

I.6: white star-topped (following HV, *LB*)] white and star-topped)

(*Editor's Note:* The HV version reads "white star-topped," as does the first appearance in 1915 *Others* and later printings, including *LB*.)

I.7: sown (following HV, *LB*)] sewn

(*Editor's Note:* The HV reads "sown," as does 1915 *Others* and later printings, including *LB*.)

I.8: Bengal (following HV and OED)] bengal

(*Editor's Note:* A Bengal light, in nineteenth-century usage, was a firework or flare used for signals, producing a steady and vivid blue light.)

III.5: spill'd (following HV and OED)] spill't

(Editor's Note: In 1993, Angela Coon adapted this section (III) for performance by the spoken-word band Bloodfest [San Francisco].)

III.7: daily news (following HV)] daily-news

IV.11: sarsenet] sarsanet

V. 14: don't] dont

IX.6: spermatozoa] spermatazoa

X.1: (*Editor's Note:* "shuttlecock and battledore" would be the correct OED spellings, but I assume that ML is deliberately punning here. Her spelling stands.)

XIX.3: (*Editor's Note:* "QHU" remains the most successful poser in ML's entire lexicon. Its meaning, if any, has so far resisted extraction. I once suspected it was an acronym, or a pun disguised as one, along the lines of Marcel Duchamp's L.H.O.O.Q. (1920). But no appositive word or translation has yet occurred that convincingly deconstructs the anagram, homograph, or rune that stands behind the upper-case construction. "QHU" may allude to an enchoric name or retronym that was once familiar but has since passed from currency. If so, perhaps some future reader will one day open the *lettre de cachet* and report its contents. Until then, it remains pure vocable or sonant, a precarious precursor of Lettrisme.

We can also imagine it as an unbroken cryptogram or enciphered message to Joannes or one of his representatives. In this case, we can only hope that GP grasped its esoteric meaning. It is also possible, more prosaically, that QHU was a printer's error, the first half of an uncorrected etaoin shrdlu [sic], or an ersatz euphemism designed to escape the censor's scythe. This pre-digital encryption recently attained electronic status. In 1995 "QHU" was posted as a query to the poetry café of the Internet community. As of now, QHU remains simply an unsolved metaplasm. The virtual café remains open to any latecomers bearing solutions: conover@mit.edu.)

XXVIII. 18: cymophanous] cymophonous

XXIX. 11: caressive] carressive

XXIX.28: (*Editor's Note:* The correct spelling would be "incognitos," but I have chosen not to emend in favor of Januzzi's enchanting suggestion that this may echo the "philosophers toes" passage in another poem featuring GP [see n. 8]. It is also possible that a pun is intended here; i.e., a low-down, toe-to-toe orgasm.)

XXX.6: archetypal] architypal

XXXIV.1: litterateur (following OED] literateur

Page breaks in 1917 *Others* occur at these lines, sometimes making stanza breaks ambiguous. Based on sense, HV, and *LB*, I have decided that 1917 page breaks do not always coincide with stanza breaks, but do in these instances (marked by *), and have lineated the present text accordingly:

II:5/6 (man / To)
*IV:8/9 (hair / One)
XIII: 25/26: (me / Or)
XVIII: 2/3: (hill / The)
*XIX: 22/23: (light / You)
XXII: 4/5: (revival / Upon)
XXIV: 6/7: (lies / Muddled)
XXVI: 2/3: (eyes / We)
XXVIII: 4/5: (Forever / Coloured)
*XXIX: 4/5: (Similitude / Unnatural)
*XXIX: 29/30: (orgasm / For)
XXXI: 2/3: (busy-body / Longing)

In imaginative terms "Joannes" is probably a figure collaged out of ML's failed relationships with several male lovers. In biographical terms he is most closely patterned after one—GP ("Joannes" translates to "Giovanni" in Italian). Following her fallout with GP (see n. 8) after an enthrallment that lasted over a year, ML confessed to CVV [n.d., 1915] that "love has calmed down to the thing that exists—'Joannes' is the most astounding creature that ever lived— in the light of my imagination. . . . I believe he's really tried to forgive me . . . & I think he's a little jealous of Songs to Joannes—an unexpected effect—".

The last page of the HV (1915) contains a note to CVV indicating that "Love Songs" (I–IV) may also have been written with an earlier lover in mind: "My dear Carlo these . . . are subconscious impressions of *8 years ago* . . . associated with my weeping willow man." This speculation is supported by her indication elsewhere (CVVP) that "Love Songs" (I–IV) were begun in a state of dysthemia ("the first were written in red-hot agony").

In 1907, eight years before ML wrote this letter to CVV, she gave birth to her second child. Burke's biography (*Becoming Modern: The Life of Mina Loy* [New York: Farrar Straus Giroux, 1996]) contains important information on SH and the filiation of this child. Its patrilineage may explain ML's agony and disillusion with GP.

Recent ML scholarship has greatly enhanced both the textual and contextual reading of this poem. See especially the work of Burke, Linda Kennahan, Kouidis, and Rachel Blau DuPlessis cited in Januzzi's bibliography of ML in *Mina Loy: Woman and Poet* (Maeera Schreiber and Keith Tuma, eds. [Orono, ME: National Poetry Foundation, 1996]).

III. Corpses and Geniuses
(Poems 1919–1930)

16. O HELL, ca. 1919. First published in *Contact* 1 (December 1920, p. 7). Reprinted in *LB*, with one substantive change: "the dusts of a tradition" replaces "the tatters of tradition" (l. 7). The present text follows the first published appearance, which in turn follows the only surviving MS (YCAL) in all substantives. I have made one emendation to the *Contact* appearance:

9: Caress] Carress

Editor's Note: When this poem was published in *Contact*, edited by RM and WCW, it marked the third time (following appearances in *Rogue* and *Others*) that ML's work had appeared in the inaugural issue of an American magazine dedicated to experimental writing. Following the demise of *Others* in 1919, WCW launched *Contact* in order to continue the fight that AK's magazine had begun. WCW sought work that could not be published elsewhere, that was not derivative, and that was not trying to appeal to good taste or win posthumous praise: "We wish above all things to speak for the present." The first issue contained two contributions by ML: "O Hell" and a prose vignette ("Summer Night in a Florentine Slum"). The prose contribution is not included in this edition (but was reprinted in *LLB*82). A variation of l. 6 ("our person is a covered entrance to infinity") occurred in ML's pamphlet *Psycho-Democracy* (Florence: Tipografia Peri & Rossi, 1920) as " 'Self' is the covered entrance to Infinity." This prose answer to FTM's *War, the World's Only Hygiene* and renunciation of Futurism's militant tenets was later reprinted in *The Little Review* 7 (Autumn 1921), pp. 14–19.

17. THE DEAD, ca. 1919. NOMS. First published in *Others for 1919: An Anthology of the New Verse* (New York: Nicholas L. Brown, 1920, pp. 112–114). This text is based on the first published appearance.

3: shrivable] shrivvable

30: Of] of

43: Has] has

Editor's Note: A year after the appearance of AK's 1919 anthology, John Rodker wrote an opinion piece in *The Little Review* 7:3 (pp. 53–56), consisting largely of sarcastic remarks about the writing of the "Others" group. Of ML's contribution Rodker quipped, "It is painful to notice that since the last 'Others' she appears to have lost her grip." ML responds thrust for thrust in the same issue.

The exchange continues in the next issue (*LR* 7:4). Harriet Monroe, reviewing this anthology in *Poetry* (17:3 [December 1920, pp. 150–158]) calls ML "an extreme otherist, as innocent of all innocences as of commas, periods, sentences. A knowing one, but we would rather have some other other's polish our stars."

Twenty-five years later, Kenneth Rexroth reprinted this poem in full in the second of his "recovery" essays on neglected poets (*Circle* 1:4 [1944, pp. 69–72]). ML had not been published anywhere for thirteen years, and he wanted something done about it: "It is hard to say why she has been ignored. Perhaps it is due to her extreme exceptionalism. Erotic poetry is usually lyric. Hers is elegiac and satirical. It is usually fast-paced. Hers is slow and deliberately twisting." Rexroth went on to observe that she "has been singularly isolated historically, with few ancestors and less influence." He named Herondas, Menander, Lucretius, Lucian, Maximinian, Marston, Donne, Jonson, and Rochester as possible precursors; he then listed Jack Wheelwright, Laura Riding, Carl Rakosi, Louis Zukofsky, and Harry Roskolenko as possible heirs. According to Rexroth, that was the complete genealogy of influence. At least, he concluded, "no others occur to me."

18. MEXICAN DESERT, ca. 1919–1920. First published in *The Dial* 70: 6 (June 1921, p. 672). There are two MSS of this poem at YCAL. This version follows the first published text, which in turn follows the MSS in all substantives.

Editor's Note: This poem is a collaged recollection of ML's traverse of the parched Mexican desert in 1918 with her second husband, AC (né Fabian Avenarius Lloyd, 1887–?). It was also her first poem to appear in *The Dial*, although her anti-Futurist play, *The Pamperers*, had inaugurated its "Modern Forms" section the year before (69:1, July 1920, pp. 65–78). Some of ML's artwork was also published in *The Dial* as *Two Watercolours* (70:4, April 1921, n.p.) and *Baby's Head* (72:2, February 1922, n.p.).

The Dial during this period was nominally edited by Scofield Thayer and Gilbert Seldes, but Scofield's co-owner, Sibley Watson, and his foreign editor, Ezra Pound, were both more editorially influential than Seldes. It is likely that Pound directed ML's first work to *The Dial*. Thayer first met ML in New York. When he encountered her again in Vienna, he recognized how valuable her knowledge of the contemporary European art scene could be to the development of the "International Art Portfolio," a project that was never fully realized but led to the publication of *Living Art* (1923). In a letter dated March 5, 1922, to Sibley Watson, Thayer referred to ML as his "assistant" in the portfolio project, thereby associating her with one of *The Dial*'s most ambitious projects (Walter Sutton, ed., *Pound, Thayer, Watson & The Dial: A Story in Letters* [Gainesville: University Press of Florida, 1994], p. 234).

The Dial was one of the most prominent literary magazines ever published in the United States. Its championing of modern artistic movements was a potent factor in shaping American taste during the 1920s. In its sponsorship of avant-garde work, it was decades ahead of popular taste. It was also one of the few solvent periodicals of its time, and one of the few which paid its contributors.

19. PERLUN, ca. July 1921. NOMS. First published in *The Dial* 71: 2 (August 1921, p. 142). This text follows the first publication.

    26: I'm] i'm

Editor's Note: The date of composition is conjectural, but the references to Dempsey and Carpentier suggest that this poem was probably written around the time of the much-publicized first million-dollar prizefight in the history of boxing. On July 21, 1921, Jack Dempsey (1895–1983) of the United States defeated Georges Carpentier (1894–1975) of France for the world heavyweight title. "Perlun" shares a number of qualities with another boxer, the eternal adolescent and heavyweight legend AC, poet-pugilist-provocateur. AC vaporized, drowned, or otherwise disappeared in Mexico in 1918, but his "pert blond spirit" seems to resurface here. Perlun's "immaculate arms," his traffic with sailors and vamps, his parasitic life-style, his detestation of the idle rich, and his instinctual, rebellious, challenging nature all call to mind AC, who as a teenage runaway worked his way aboard freighters and trains from Europe to Australia to California, where he rode boxcars with hoboes and picked lemons with migrant laborers. In an unpublished prose memoir, ML eulogized AC as "Colossus," identified in Greek mythology with Helios, brother of Selene, goddess of the moon. Elsewhere she identified him with Mercury, Roman god of eloquence, thievery, and travel. Excerpts of her memoir appear in Roger L. Conover's "Mina Loy's Colossus: Arthur Cravan Undressed," Rudolf E. Kuenzli, ed., *New York Dada* ([New York: Willis Locker & Owens, 1986], pp. 102–19). Selections of AC's writings appear in *Four Dada Suicides* ([London: Atlas Press, 1995], pp. 33–88).

Alternatively, the mysteriously named title figure of this poem may come to us *per luna*. Or he may be named for one of his habits; like AC, who boasted that he was a thief, Perlun purloins.

A final note: Francis Picabia printed a doctored portrait of boxer Georges Carpentier on the cover of *391* (October 1924), deliberately passing it off as a portrait of Marcel Duchamp, to whom Carpentier bore a striking resemblance. Thus Carpentier shares with AC the distinction of being the only boxers featured in Dada's most international and adventuresome journal.

20. POE. Composition date unknown, but in all likelihood this poem postdates AC's disappearance in 1918. NOMS. First published in *The Dial* 1:4 (October 1921, p. 406). Reprinted in *LB* ("1921–1922") without changes. This text follows the first publication.

9: "ilix" is an uncommon but accepted (OED) spelling of "ilex," the ever-green shrub, or holm oak.

21. APOLOGY OF GENIUS, ca. 1922. First published in *The Dial* 73 (July 1922, pp. 73–74). Reprinted in *LB* without changes. No MS has been located, but a fragmentary draft of a sequel, "Apology of Genius II," dated 1930, is among ML's papers at YCAL. Reprinted in *LB* without substantive changes. The text of this frequently anthologized poem follows the first published version, except for the following emendations:

13: fools'] fool's

37: immortelles] immortels

(According to the OED, "immortelles" are various composite flowers of papery texture which retain their color and shape after being cut and dried. Immortelles are commonly used to adorn gravestones and tombs. ML wore them in her hats. Here she evokes them in praise of artistic genius.)

Editor's Note: This was one of two works by ML which YW felt "need, in [his] judgment, yield ground to no one." The other was "Der Blinde Junge" (see n. 24). YW's essay is one of the first significant attempts to come to terms with ML's work, both on its own terms and in relation to that of her contemporaries; the only significant prior attempt was EP's review of the 1917 *Others* anthology in which he first took up ML and MM (n. 9). Winters concluded that ML had more to offer than Moore and Stevens, and is "one of the two living poets who have the most . . . to offer the younger American writers." WCW was the other. Of the four poets, YW found ML's achievement "by all odds the most astound-ing. Using an unexciting method, and writing of the drabbest of material, she has written seven or eight of the most brilliant and unshakably solid satirical poems of our time, and at least two non-satirical pieces that possess . . . a beauty that is unspeakably moving and profound." Of all the modernists, he declared WCW and ML the two who "present us with a solid foundation in place of Whitman's badly aligned corner-stones, a foundation which is likely to be employed, I suspect, by a generation or two. . . . If it materializes, Emily Dickinson will have been its only forerunner." YW's essay bears read-ing in its entirety (Yvor Winters, "Mina Loy," *The Dial* 70, June 1926, pp. 496–99). His assessment stands in sharp counterpoint to Harriet Monroe's review of *LB*:

Mostly, her utterance is a condescension from a spirit too burdened with expe-rience to relax the ironic tension of her grasp upon it. The load being too heavy to talk about, she carries it as she may . . . making gay little satiric moues as she passes, and giving forth sardonic little cries.

(*Poetry* 23:2 [November 1923], pp. 100–3)

"Apology of Genius" was ML's first poem translated into French. NCB was so moved by ML's May 6, 1927, reading at her 20, rue Jacob salon that she later translated this poem and published it in her memoirs (*Aventures de l'Esprit*

[Paris: Editions Emile-Paul Frères, 1929], pp. 213–16), along with an account of the poet reading it:

Her beauty has withdrawn into itself. She offers us this "apology of genius," and an entire prismatic poetry which, thanks to some perception of a fourth destiny, she escapes.

(Translation by John Spalding Gatton, ed., NCB: Adventures of the Mind *[New York: NYU Press, 1992], pp. 100–3)*

22. BRANCUSI'S GOLDEN BIRD, 1922. First published in the *The Dial* 73 (November 1922, pp. 507–8), opposite CB's studio photograph of the *Golden Bird*. The same image had previously been reproduced in the "Brancusi" number of *The Little Review* 8 (Autumn 1921, pl. 17) accompanying EP's essay on CB. A typescript in WAA appears to be a copy of the *Dial* text transcribed by Arensberg. Reprinted in *LB* ("1921–1922"). This text follows the first published version, to which I have made one correction:

    28: aggressive] agressive

Editor's Note: This is one of two works by ML featuring CB (1876–1957). The other, a pencil portrait of the sculptor's head, is reproduced in *LLB82* (pl. 18). Although ML and CB would later become friends in Paris, and appear in photographs with Jane Heap, Margaret Anderson, and Tristan Tzara, "when she wrote this poem she had never met the Rumanian genius of sculpture . . . the poem represents a real intuitional appreciation" (Eugene Jolas, *Paris Tribune*, July 24, 1924). ML's poem is among the first "American" appreciations of CB's work. Along with Henry McBride, she was the first writer to champion Brancusi in *The Dial*.

ML's sixth and final contribution to *The Dial* appeared in the magazine's famous *Waste Land* issue. The magazine quickly sold out its sixteen thousand copies and prompted a vituperative exchange between Scofield Thayer and his managing editor, Gilbert Seldes. Thayer objected to the reproduction of CB's photograph on the grounds that it had "no aesthetic value whatever" and was "commercially suicidal." Seldes shot back that it was ML's poem, not CB's photograph, that caused "the only row . . . in that connection." These events preceded by several years the legal dispute over whether CB's *Bird in Space* should be allowed to pass through customs duty-free (as art) or should be considered a piece of metalwork and therefore be subject to import tax as an object of manufacture. This controversy (decided by the Customs Court in CB's favor) preceded by only one year the dispute over whether ML's first book (*LB*) should be able to pass through customs at all, and may partially explain the radical revisions she made to "Songs to Joannes" between its first periodical appearance and its reconstitution in book form as "Love Songs" (n. 15).

Many CB scholars have cited this poem, and it has been reprinted in several books and catalogues on CB, including the historically significant catalogue for his first major one-person show in New York (Brummer Gallery, 1926). All

CB literature to date has identified the *Golden Bird* of ML's title as the celebrated 1919 bronze sculpture purchased by lawyer, patron, and collector John Quinn (1870–1924), now owned by the Art Institute of Chicago. This claim was most recently made by Margherita Androeotti in her essay "Brancusi's *Golden Bird*: A New Species of Modern Sculpture" (Art Institute of Chicago, *Museum Studies*, 19:3, pp. 134–52). Androeotti is correct in speculating that ML could easily have seen the sculpture in either the home of Quinn or at the exhibition "Contemporary French Art" (Sculptors' Gallery, New York, 1922). These circumstances, coupled with the photograph of the canonical *Golden Bird* which accompanied the first appearance of the poem, make a convenient case to support this theory. But they do not take into account another fact: that there was a second *Golden Bird* produced at roughly the same time (1919–20), which was nearly identical to the first in size, form, and materials. Both are listed in Friedrich Teja Bach's definitive catalogue raisonné, *Constantin Brancusi* (Dumont: Cologne, 1987) under the French heading *l'Oiseau d'Or* (cf. entries 155 and 156, pp. 456–57).

The less known of the two (now in the collection of the Minneapolis Institute of Arts) was originally purchased on December 16, 1921 (for 5,000 francs), by Mariette Mills, the expatriate American sculptor and former student of French sculptor Antoine [Émile] Bourdelle. In the summer of 1921, ML visited her close friends Mariette and Heyworth Mills in their home on rue Boissonnade, where she had an epiphanic encounter with the bronze sculpture. ML recorded her first reaction to the *Golden Bird* in her 1950 essay "Phenomenon in American Art" (YCAL/*LLB*82): "Years ago at wonderful Mariette Mills' I came face to face, or rather face to flight with Brancusi's Bird." She then described the "long aesthetic itinerary from Brancusi's Golden Bird to [Joseph] Cornell's Aviary," calling CB's sculpture "the purest abstraction I have ever seen." Given the resemblance of the two sculptures, ML could have been responding to either "aesthetic archetype." But her written recollection strongly suggests that she was writing not about Quinn's *Golden Bird* but rather about the less celebrated *Golden Bird* that she saw at the Millses' (Bach 156).

23. LUNAR BAEDEKER. Date of composition unknown; *LB* "1921–1922" opens with this poem, marking its first appearance. NOMS. The present text follows the first published version.

title: Lunar Baedeker] Lunar Baedecker

8: In Persian mythology "peris" are fairies or elves descended from evil angels and barred from Paradise until they have served penance for their forebears' sins.

10: In Greek and Roman mythology, Lethe is the river of forgetfulness, flowing through Hades, whose water produced memory loss in those who drank it.

15: Infusoria are microscopic organisms found in decayed organic matter.

38: oxidized] oxidised

Editor's Note: All collected and selected editions of ML's poems to date have been named after this corner-poem, the first by her choice, the rest in memory of her ill-starred first book, *Lunar Baedecker* [*sic*]. Whatever pleasure ML experienced upon seeing her first book published must have been immediately compromised when she realized that the title was misspelled, not only on the cover, but on the half-title page, title page, and first page of the book. Notwithstanding this lapse, publication by RM's Contact Press placed ML in select expatriate company. Appearing under the same imprint were first or early books by Ernest Hemingway, WCW, GS, Marsden Hartley, Mary Butts, H.D., and Emanuel Carnevali.

This poem was recently adapted by composer Sebastian Anthony Birch for a musical work entitled "Argentum" (Cleveland Museum of Art, 1994); it is also the first of ML's poems to be released in CD-ROM format (Fiorella Terenzi, ed., *The Invisible Universe* [New York: Voyager Press, 1995]).

24. DER BLINDE JUNGE, ca. 1922. NOMS. First published in *LB* ("1921–1922" section), immediately preceding "Ignoramus." This text follows the *LB* version.

title: "Der Blinde Junge" translates from German to "The Blind Youth."

1: In Roman mythology, "Bellona" is the goddess of war, sister of Mars.

4: "Kreigsopfer" is a German compound noun meaning "war victim."

12: its] it's

18: lightning] lightening

28: "Illuminati," plural of "illuminato," originally referred to certain religious sects, but in modern usage it refers to any persons claiming special knowledge or enlightenment. In its later sense, it is often used ironically (OED), as is the case here.

Editor's Note: This poem made an immediate and lasting impression on YW, who considered it among ML's best poems when he first discussed her work in 1926 (n. 21). Some forty years later, he reaffirmed his early estimation of this poem. By this time ML's work was all but forgotten, but YW was still convinced of its lasting value (*Forms of Discovery* [Chicago: Alan Swallow, 1967], n.d., n.p.). Between these first and last impressions, YW had issued a mid-career advisory that was less approving: "Mina Loy's verse is usually so simplified, so denuded of secondary accent, as to be indistinguishable from prose" (*Primitivism and Decadence* [Arrow Editions, 1937]), a description surprisingly close to Monroe's characterization of ML's work as "descriptive, explanatory, philosophic—in short, prose, which no amount of radical empiricism, in the sound and exclamatory arrangement of words and lines, can transform, with prestidigitatorial magic, into the stuff of poetry" (*Poetry*, November 1923).

Thom Gunn's consideration of this poem, from which I quote only a brief passage, deserves to be read in its entirety:

Loy is a tough writer, and sentiment in the usual sense is seldom present in her work. Her overt feeling in ["Der Blinde Junge"] is of contempt, turned upon the rest of us, the illuminati reading her poem, complacently assuming that we are heirs to culture. . . . She is hard, pure, unrelenting. The controlled anger and indignation of the poem make it the equal, to my mind, of the best of Pope or Swift.

("Three Hard Women: HD, Marianne Moore, Mina Loy," in Vereen Bell and Laurence Lerner, eds., On Modern Poetry *[Nashville: Vanderbilt University Press, 1988])*

25. CRAB-ANGEL. Composition date unknown. NOMS. First published in *LB* ("1921–1922"). This text follows the *LB* version, except for the following emendations:

    8, 19: its] it's

    21: iridescent] irridescent

    40: up-a-loft] up-a-flot

    (While "flot" is an obsolete form of "float" and "up-afloat" could be what ML intended, I have emended to "up-a-loft," largely on the strength of Jim Powell's suggestion that "up-a-loft" is a pseudo-archaic, poetical locution for "air, as in theatrical space.")

    52: lightning] lightening

26. JOYCE'S ULYSSES. Composition date unknown. NOMS. First published in *LB* ("1921–1922"). This text follows the first published version, with the exception of two emendations:

    24: satirize] satirise

    44: its] it's

Editor's Note: This poem was probably written shortly after the publication of the first edition of James Joyce's *Ulysses* (February 1922) by Sylvia Beach's Shakespeare & Company Bookshop, but possibly earlier. ML closely monitored the events preceding its publication, namely, the confiscation and destruction by the U.S. Post Office of four issues of *The Little Review* in which serial installments of the novel had appeared between 1918 and 1921. Attorney-collector John Quinn (n. 22, 27) tried unsuccessfully to defend the magazine's editors in court. Shortly after ML met Joyce in Paris, her portrait of him appeared in *Vanity Fair* (April 1922, p. 65).

27. "THE STARRY SKY" OF WYNDHAM LEWIS. Composition date unknown. NOMS. First published in *LB* ("1921–1922"), but probably written somewhat earlier, following the reproduction of Lewis's *The Starry Sky* (pencil,

pen, ink, wash, and gouache drawing, 1912) in the November 1917 issue of *The Little Review*. This edition's text follows the first published appearance.

Editor's Note: Wyndham Lewis (1884–1957), the English painter, writer, and iconoclast, became famous for aiming invective at the Bloomsbury group ("pansy-clan") in the pages of his polemical puce-colored magazine, *Blast*, while ML was still in Florence. Like FTM, Lewis was the impresario of an aggressive cultural reform movement, in his case, Vorticism, which assaulted guardians of taste and advocated the overthrow of outmoded institutions and traditions. Vorticism advocated violence against Victorianism and celebrated the vortex as the point of maximum energy, concentration, and power. ML had known Lewis in Paris, had been impressed by his "Timon of Athens" series in the Second Post-Impressionist Exhibition in London (1912), and had followed his arguments with FTM. Finally, after seeing his work in a second exhibition at the Grafton Galleries in London (1914), she reintroduced herself as "an old friend of the Montparnasse quarter—Mina Haweis—" then made some polite remarks about the show, before letting go: "Of all the new work which seems to be groping in super-consciousness—yours alone is creating there—masterfully aware. . . . I am rash—but please tell me what the drawings cost—I must . . . have one" (WL).

The name of the drawing celebrated in this poem was keyed to a footnote in *LB*: "a drawing in the collection of John Quinn." John Quinn, one of the prime forces behind the 1913 Armory Show, at one time owned Lewis's *The Starry Sky*, Brancusi's *Golden Bird*, and the manuscript of Joyce's *Ulysses*. All three works were featured in *The Little Review*, and all three were the subjects of poems by ML (see n. 22, 26).

Scofield Thayer once recommended to his partner, Sibley Watson, that WL's *Starry Heavens* be included in the "International Art Portfolio" project of *The Dial* (see n. 18); in the same letter (March 5, 1922), he suggested that Mr. Quinn's "vanity should be played upon by the mention that his name as a patron of contemporary art would appear in the preface to this folio. . . . I myself should write a short preface giving names of the artists . . . and mentioning the name of my assistant Alfred [Kreymborg] or Mina [Loy]" (Sutton, *Pound, Thayer, Watson, & The Dial*, p. 234).

28. MARBLE, 1923. This poem was published in a prospectus announcing the formation of a new journal, the Paris-based *transatlantic review* (n.d., 1923), edited by FMF (1873–1939). The text of the present edition follows the first and only known published version (ENC), which differs from the HV (CU) only in the deletion of dashes after ll. 13 and 14. Early drafts of this poem are preserved at YCAL.

Editor's Note: In planning his new "exile" magazine, *transatlantic review*, FMF sent a limited number of gratis copies of a "Preliminary Number" to influential friends and prospective subscribers. In it, he listed the writers and previewed the work that his new venture would support: TSE, RM, Mary Butts, James Joyce, E. E. Cummings, EP, and ML were among the writers named. Most of the sample poems printed in the prospectus later appeared in official numbers of the magazine; ML's was one of only three that did not. "Marble" is thus among the most obscure of Loy's published poems. Its existence was noted by Bernard J. Poli in *Ford Madox Ford and the Transatlantic Review* (Syracuse University Press, 1967, p. 42).

29. GERTRUDE STEIN, ca. 1924. NOMS. First published in 1924 as an untitled epigraph to a two-part letter in which ML discusses the influences on and maieutic effects of GS's compositional techniques. ML's prose statement (reprinted in *LLB82*) ran in two successive installments of *transatlantic review* (2:3 [October, pp. 305–9]; 2:4 [November, pp. 427–30]) under the title "Gertrude Stein," GS's novel, *The Making of Americans*, was serialized in *tr* the same year (1924). This text follows the poem's first published appearance, with the exception of the title, which I have supplied.

Editor's Note: ML's description of GS also applies to her own literary exercise: "a most dexterous discretion in the placement and replacement of . . . phrases" by an "uncompromised intellect [who] has scrubbed the meshed messes of traditional associations off them." At one point in her narrative, ML prospects her own epigraph, describing the "incoherent debris . . . littered around the radium that [GS] crushes out of phrased conssciousness."

On February 4, 1927, GS was the featured speaker at NCB's salon. ML was asked to introduce her, and in doing so she drew again on her poem. "Je vous présente Gertrude Stein . . . la madame Curie du langage" (*Aventures de L'Esprit*, p. 233). Harold Loeb, editor of *Broom*, recalled in his autobiography that ML once offered him an essay that accounted for the obscurity of GS's prose by suggesting that "the author was providing merely a framework upon which the reader could erect whatever superstructure was congenial." He was probably referring to the essay later accepted by FMF, in which ML insisted that the art of GS, "like all modern art . . . leaves an unlimited latitude for personal response" (*The Way It Was* [New York: Criterion Books, 1959], p. 129).

In *The Autobiography of Alice B. Toklas* (New York: Harcourt Brace, 1933, p. 162) GS paid tribute to ML's perceptive readings of her unpublished manuscripts, praising in particular her ability "to understand without the commas." As for Toklas herself, she remembered ML as "beautiful, intelligent, sympathetic and gay" (*What Is Remembered* [New York: Holt, Rinehart and Winston], p. 76).

30. THE WIDOW'S JAZZ, 1927. First published in *Pagany: A Native Quarterly*, 2:2 (Spring 1931, pp. 18–20). There is an early draft of this poem at YCAL, but no finished MS has been found. The text of the present edition follows the first published version, with the exception of line 29, where "Cra-

ven" has been emended to "Cravan." ML is invoking by name her missing husband, AC, the subject of the poet's monodic address later in the poem (l. 39–40).

Editor's Note: In her memoirs, NCB provides a vivid account of ML's first public reading of this "just completed" poem at her salon. In preparation for the May 6, 1927, reading, ML worked out with her personal trainer "in the solitude of [NCB's] second floor." NCB was quite impressed that a poet should put herself through warm-up exercises before a literary performance, with the support of "a trainer such as boxers have" (NCB, pp. 213–16). Djuna Barnes attended the reading, and later wrote a fictional satire of NCB's salon in which ML appears as the elusive "Patience Scalpel," whose ankles "are nibbled by Cherubs" (*The Ladies Almanack* [Paris: Edward W. Tltus, 1928]). In NCB's autobiographical account, ML is described walking "as though the angels were already nibbling at her heels."

On September 25, 1927, ML sent a copy of this poem and "Lady Laura in Bohemia" (n. 31) to her daughter Joella, who had recently married Julien Levy and moved to New York: "*Would* you take it round to the *Dial*—with my love to Thayer and Marianne Moore and let them see whether they want one of them. . . . I don't know what to *write* to them—in fact I don't know which of them it is polite to address—don't know who's who in the buyer's department. Do do that little thing for me. Am I not a bore?" (MLL).

It is not known whether MM or Thayer ever saw these poems, but in 1930 Julien Levy was asked by Richard Johns if he could supply some photographs by Eugene Atget for publication in his new magazine, *Pagany*. Levy obliged, then asked a favor of his own. Would Johns consider publishing two of his mother-in-law's poems? Shortly thereafter (n.d., 1930) Levy wrote to ML victoriously: "A new magazine called *Pagany* received my permission on behalf of Mina Loy to announce the forthcoming publication of one or two of your poems ["The Widow's Jazz" and "Lady Laura in Bohemia"]. It isn't at all a bad magazine, publishing Billy Williams, Gertrude Stein, Mary Butts. . . . *Much* more exclusive than *Transition*, more alive than the recent *Dials*, and less conceited than the *Hound and Horn*. Won't you send me some more recent work than those two that I have?" (JL).

The contributor's note in *Pagany* announced: "Mina Loy, of the Others group, is writing poetry again after several years' silence." Indeed, with the exception of "Gertrude Stein", which was superscribed to an essay, ML had not published anywhere for nine years.

Pagany was launched by Richard Johns in 1930, with the editorial support of WCW. It announced itself as "a speculative venture, filling in the middle scene between the excellent conventional magazines and those which are entirely experimental in content." It folded in 1933.

31. LADY LAURA IN BOHEMIA. Composition date unknown, but by reference to the letter quoted in the previous note it is clear that this poem was completed by 1927. NOMS. First published in *Pagany* 2:3 (Summer 1931, pp. 125–27). The present text follows the first published appearance, where page breaks occur between lines 12 and 13 and 44 and 45; in the present edition, these are also stanza breaks.

Editor's Note: "Zelli's" (l. 27) was a well-known bar in Montparnasse frequented by ML and her fellow expatriates in the 1920s. Llike "Ignoramus" (n. 13), this poem anticipates the later destitution poems of ML's Bowery period (Section 4). After the publication of this poem, ML did not publish again until 1946—the longest silence of her career.

32. THE MEDITERRANEAN SEA, ca. 1928. First published in *LLB*82, p. 250. There is a signed, undated typescript at YCAL, which serves as the basis for the present text; I have made several emendations to it:

    22: Lacrimae] Lacrimi
    23: imperceptibly] imperceptably
    25: Apuane] Appuane
    (Carrara, a region of Italy famous for its marble, sits in the Apuane Alps.)

33. NANCY CUNARD. Composition date unknown, probably late 1920s. First published in *LLB*82, p. 259. The present text follows the signed typescript at YCAL, to which I have made three emendations:

    3: helmeted] helmetted
    6: vermilion] vermillion
    7: receding] receeding

Editor's Note: NC (1896–1965), rebel-heiress-seductress-poet, was one of the stormiest and most colorful figures of 1920s Paris. Her temperamental extremes and controversial stands were often limned—unflatteringly—in the fiction of her ex-lovers. Three of them—Aldous Huxley, Michael Arlen and Louis Aragon—featured characters based on her in novels. She also made cameo appearances in the fiction of Evelyn Waugh and Richard Aldington. It has long been hypothesized, although inconclusively, that she was the inspiration for Lady Brett Ashley in Ernest Hemingway's *The Sun Also Rises*, and it has also been suggested that she modelled for Fresca in TSE's drafts for "The Fire Sermon" section of *The Waste Land*, a speculation which does not serve either TSE's or NC's reputation well. TSE's portrait of a spoiled society girl with literary ambitions reveals a "powerful disgust for Fresca's sexuality and contempt for her poetic dabblings. Intellectual women, he states, are even less interesting than ordinary sluts. Beneath their pretensions, there is the same basic lust" (Anne Chisholm, *Nancy Cunard: A Biography* [New York: Alfred A. Knopf, 1979], p. 339).

As the founder and editor of the Hours Press, NC was Samuel Beckett's first publisher. As an avid supporter of the French Resistance, she was high on Hitler's blacklist. As an outspoken defender of the rights of American blacks, she was once banned from entering the United States. And as the debutante daughter of English shipping magnates Lady Emerald and Sir Bache Cunard, she used her money to support people and causes that made her an outcast in her own family. But it was her bewitching appearance and seductive countenance that drew so many writers' and artists' attentions to her. CB, Wyndham Lewis, Man Ray, Cecil Beaton, Oskar Kokoschka, and John Banting were among those who painted, sculpted, or photographed her.

It has been suggested that ML may have been making an ironic comment on NC's involvement with "race issues" in this poem, but this surmise strikes me as doubtful. Not only were both women sympathetic to some of the same causes, they admired many of the same artists and shared several important friends in common. Because of its careful attention to visual details and physical features, and its markedly iconographic approach to its subject throughout, I think it is far more likely that this poem was written not as a social portrait of NC but as a depiction of an actual portrait. ML was certainly aware of the extent to which NC was an artistically desirable model. This poem may well be based on a specific portrait of NC that she saw alongside portraits of George Moore and Princess Murat in NC's home on rue le Regrattier, Paris. For example, the poem follows the English Surrealist painter John Banting's likeness of NC in certain details.

Moore, the Irish novelist, was a lifelong friend of NC, who privately wondered whether she might be his daughter. It was no secret that he had had an affair with her mother, or that he took a paternal interest in the activities of NC, who late in life published a memoir about him (*G.M. : Memories of George Moore* [London: Rupert Hart-Davis, 1956]). The subject of the other portrait, Princess Murat (l. 23), raises identity questions of another sort. She could easily be the Surrealist cult figure and eccentric French princess Violette Murat, with whom René Crevel smoked opium in an abandoned submarine, just before his death in Toulon in 1930. She would have known NC. She could also be Princess Lucien Murat, friend of the Dadaists. It is more in keeping with NC's taste and ML's eye for detail to imagine a likeness of one of these figures occupying space within the frame of the painting and the poem than it is to imagine her as Princess Caroline [Bonaparte] Murat, Napoleon's sister. But that remains a *haute bourgeoise* possibility. Finally, an "American princess called Murat" turns up in Peggy Guggenheim's memoirs. This sketchily described princess rented Guggenheim's house in Pramousquier (ca. 1927–28), where ML had also been an early guest and painted a fresco on the wall of her bedroom (*Out of this Century: Confessions of an Art Addict* [New York: Universe Books, 1979], p. 93).

34. JULES PASCIN. Composed ca. June 1930. First published in *LBT*. This text follows the typescript at YCAL.

Editor's Note: This is one of two portraits that ML composed of Jules Pascin (1885–1930), the Bulgarian-born Jewish artist whose suicide sent a tremor through the Paris art world. The other is a line drawing dating from the 1920s (*LLB82*, pl. 17). ML wrote this poem following Pascin's "Portuguese" suicide (he belted his neck to a doorknob before slashing his wrists). In a letter to the Levys following Pascin's death, ML boasted: "Pascin's last words to me were that I was the only one whose poetry was equal to Valéry's—yes!" (MLL, September 10, 1930).

Later in 1930, ML wrote to the Levys again:

*"I sent Bernie Bandler [*Hound and Horn *editor Bernard Bandler II] my poem about Pascin—because he had begged me to show him something—and he didn't accept it on the spot as I expected—and at lunch I asked him surprised— apropos of something—but you do* take *things for the H&H . . . when he answered me [that] he did—I stared and gasped with amazement—then why don't you take mine? He said—I've sent it on to (someone or other)—we* both *decide— & I exclaimed—nonsense. Can't you make up your mind for yourself? And I've heard no more of him—I'm going to send some [poems] to Djuna [Barnes]. . . . Djuna wrote to me to send some as she would like to try & place some for me. These high brow magazines are dangerous trifles—of the Dial—Scofield Thayer is hopelessly mad—another of their editors is going mad—& a third is just coming out of madness. And this erstwhile contributor may be mad!" (MLL)*

IV. Compensations of Poverty
(Poems 1942–1949)

35. ON THIRD AVENUE, 1942. Parts 1 and 2 were first published together in *LLB82*; part 2 made an earlier appearance in *LBT*. Neither appeared previously in a periodical. This text follows a signed, dated MS at YCAL, with the exception of two emendations:

9: preceding] preceeding
32: its] it's

Editor's Note: "On Third Avenue" is the first in a series of poems which ML grouped in a folder (YCAL) under the working title "Compensations of Poverty." ML probably hoped to publish them as a book. In addition to "On Third Avenue" the folder contains "Ephemerid," "Chiffon Velours," "Mass-Production on 14th Street," "Child Chanting," "Property of Pigeons," "Idiot Child on a Fire-Escape," and "Aid of the Madonna," as well as several other poems which appeared in *LLB82* but are not present here.

As early as 1915, one can detect in ML's letters and poems a sympathy for and identification with tramps, addicts, and derelicts. Late in life, she wrote with as much animation about her encounters with them as she once had about her meetings with great artists and poets. In 1936 ML left Europe for the last time; she spent much of the next seventeen years moving from one communal rooming house to another in lower Manhattan and the Bowery. During this last artistically productive period of her career, she became increasingly reclusive and isolated, gradually losing touch with all but a few of her old friends. Dispossessed of the furniture and friendships of the art world, she replaced them with the castoffs and human refuse of her daily rounds. She had once enjoyed cerebral exchanges in the parlors of geniuses; now she was more comfortable exchanging cigarettes with strangers she met on the street.

By the early 1950s, Berenice Abbott, Djuna Barnes, Joseph Cornell, and Marcel Duchamp were among the few "official" visitors whose knock Loy would still acknowledge at the drab door of her shared apartment on Stanton Street. She was a kind of sidewalk saint to the loafers and indigents of her Bowery neighborhood, an ethereal white-haired figure floating past doorways with shopping bags full of cardboard and cans, offering cures for the hungover and wine for the thirsty. "Mama Mina," some called her. To others she was "the Duchess." Like a modern Saint Gilles, the legendary protector of lepers and cripples, she was generous with change, favors, and had an unlimited inventory of stories. No one knew or cared if her recollections were delusional. She was part of pedestrian ecology, part of the communal street. She held séances, worked crossword puzzles, and patented designs for curtain rods and other household inventions out of what others threw away. Her attraction to trash began in the 1900s; it preceded Dada.

She once drew portraits of the great modernist icons of her generation and trafficked in surrealist paintings; now she drew figures of shoeless demimondaines huddled in doorways and stuffed her closets with egg crates. She had once been a model and a modiste; now she wore her nightgown in the street, part of the human shuffle known as the Bowery sidewalk. She existed in the margins of the formal economy and outside the notice of official culture. She had always been an outsider, but now, as an insider in a world of outsiders, she was creating identity for a people and place as far beneath the dignity of museums as her "Love Songs" of the 1910s had been beneath the dignity of critics. When she scavenged the back alleys for flattened cans and abandoned mopheads, it was not to fashion a shelter but to create a poignant vision of shelterless existence. We will never know how many of these raw collages of homeless, angelic bums watching over the street or curled next to parking meters in innocent sleep were lost, but a number of them have been preserved as a result of a show curated by Marcel Duchamp at the Bodley Gallery in 1959. This was the last public event focused on ML until her funeral. ML did not attend the opening.

During this period, she was also writing her last poems, drawing on the same unheroic figures and streets to depict the underside of an urban environment which was now her own—a zone where panhandlers and unknown poets saw their broken dreams reflected in each other's eyes, and were constantly having to adjust themselves to the ever-shrinking boundaries of their social space. When she wrote about marginalized, discarded people precariously living their anonymous lives between pigeons and curbstones, she was not doing so with pity or disgust. She was describing the spiritual compensations of penury, perched as she was in *dishabille* at dignity's last doorway. Some of these poems feature scenes, figures, and phrases also found in her three-dimensional assemblages.

36. MASS-PRODUCTION ON 14th STREET, 1942. This text is based on the signed, dated (July 27, 1942), hand-corrected MS at YCAL. First published in *LBT*; no periodical publication.

  28: Carnevale] Carneval

  (I assume that ML was aiming for the Italian spelling, but "Carnaval" [French] is also possible here.)

  43: simulacra's] simulacres'

37. IDIOT CHILD ON A FIRE-ESCAPE, 1943. First published in *Partisan Review* 19:5 (September–October 1952, p. 561). This text follows the first published version, with the exception of two changes in punctuation: the substitution of a comma for a period after line 5 and the addition of a comma after line 6. These emendations follow ML's dated typescript (MLA), which bears a notation in her hand recording the publication in *PR*.

Editor's Note: This poem was submitted to *PR* by Levy and accepted by Philip Rahv.

38. AID OF THE MADONNA, 1943. The first three stanzas were published in *Accent* 7:4 (Winter 1947, p. 111). The *Accent* text corresponds to the first page of a signed and dated MS at YCAL, the second page of which contains three additional stanzas.

Editor's Note: In a variation from the stated editorial policy of this edition, I am following the text of the MS, on the assumption that this represents the version prepared by the author for publication. In all likelihood the second half of the poem was cut by *Accent*, or possibly by Gilbert Neiman (see n. 39). I base this assumption on the fact that ML circulated the longer version to Joseph Cornell (JC) and other friends shortly after the poem's publication, and that all six stanzas were completed prior to its first publication in 1943.

39. EPHEMERID, 1944. First published in *Accent* 6:4 (Summer 1946, pp. 240–41). This text follows the *Accent* version, which differs very slightly from the MS (YCAL) dated August 1944. The latter indicates no stanza breaks

between ll. 16 and 17 and 41 and 42, an upper-case "M" at the beginning of l. 3, and substitutes the word "Elevated" for the more colloquial "El's" in l. 5.
Editor's Note: Accent was considered one of the best of the university-based literary magazines of its era. ML's poems were sent to its editor, Kerker Quinn (then a faculty member of the University of Illinois English Department), by Gilbert Neiman, the novelist (*There Is a Tyrant in Every Country* [Harcourt Brace, 1947]). Neiman was a friend of Henry Miller and Frieda Lawrence and a longtime admirer of ML. He was not the first or last reader to express an interest verging on obsession in the poet and her work. Long before he met her, and seemingly out of nowhere, he deluged her with letters, sometimes addressing her as "the love of my youth," other times as his "preceptress." ML's poems seemed to have a talismanic effect on the young writer, operating almost as philters. Following a dinner in New York arranged by Miller, Neiman wrote (November 9, 1945): "I would like to send your poems to *Accent*. I mentioned you, and they were very interested. If you would send them to me first, I'd be able to copy a few for myself—which I'd far prefer" (GN). *Accent* accepted all four poems Neiman submitted. "Ephemerid" was the first to appear, marking ML's return to print after thirteen years.

Encouraged by his success with *Accent*, Neiman tried without success to place other poems for ML in the late 1940s and early 1950s. He was turned down by *Circle*, *Poetry*, and several other magazines. He also tried to interest his own editor at Harcourt Brace in publishing a collection of her poems, possibly "Compensations of Poverty", in 1947.

40. CHIFFON VELOURS, 1944. First published in *Accent* 7:4 (Winter 1947, p. 112). The present text follows the *Accent* version, which varies from the draft MS dated May 6, 1944 (YCAL) only in accidentals (comma at the end of l. 16, dashes at end of l. 21 and beginning of l. 22).
Editor's Note: These variations could well have been introduced by Neiman, who wrote ML on November 23, 1945: "I've promised Accent I would send the poems of yours. I'll type off a few" (GN).

41. PROPERTY OF PIGEONS. Composition date unknown. First published in *Between Worlds: An International Magazine of Creativity* 1:2 (Spring/Summer 1961, pp. 203–4). I have made several emendations to the *BW* text, based on ML's hand-corrected MSS at YCAL and GN, which clearly establish her wishes at the time of publication:
    27: frowardly] forwardly
    32: to] of
    33/34: no stanza break
    37: a] A
    44: intestate] interstate
Editor's Note: In 1960 Neiman, who had last written to ML in 1945, wrote to

her again, this time from his new post at the Inter-American University of Puerto Rico:

We are starting a magazine that has as its goal the rapprochement of creative writers of the East and the West, on the basis of creative art and not creative physics. It will have no politics whatsoever, no criticisms and no book reviews. . . . We will print the work of young writers in the so-called growth areas: Puerto Rico, the West Indies, Ghana, India, Japan, all of Central and South America. Alongside these newcomers we want to print famous writers from the great creative movements of our time: Dadaists, Surrealists, Existentialists, and even a few Beatniks. . . . It would be of inestimable help to us, and especially to me, a great pleasure to be able to print something of yours."

ML apparently responded, for on September 8 of the same year GN thanked her for her letter: "Even though you don't seem to remember me . . . I feel as devoted to your poetry . . . as I did at a starry-eyed sixteen, when I decided that Sandburg didn't have all the answers" (GN).

Neiman published seven poems by ML in his new magazine; they were the last poems she published anywhere during her lifetime. With the exception of the *Partisan Review* appearance in 1952 and the publication of "Aviator's Eyes" in an obscure article by Larry Krantz ("Three Neglected Poets," *Wagner Literary Magazine* [Spring 1959, p. 54]), Neiman was responsible, directly or indirectly, for every periodical appearance ML made after 1931. The last two poems that she would live to see published both appeared in the pages of his magazine. She was eighty. Neiman's effort is remarkable only because it indicates how different the published record might have been had other editors taken similar initiatives. When Neiman expressed interest in ML's work, she obliged. It didn't matter that she had no recollection of meeting him or that he was writing on behalf of an offshore magazine of no standing. In 1961, ML's name would certainly have been unfamiliar to most readers of *BW*, but that didn't keep Neiman from announcing ML's work in oracular terms on the inside front cover: "poems by the sibyl of the century."

Jim Powell has provided a most elegant and inspired elucidation of this poem in "Basil Bunting and Mina Loy," *Chicago Review* 37:1 (Winter 1990, pp. 6–25).

42. PHOTO AFTER POGROM, ca. 1945. First published in *Between Worlds* 1:2 (Spring/Summer 1961, p. 201). This text follows the *BW* version, which in turn follows ML's hand-corrected MS (YCAL) in all substantives.
Editor's Note: Readers who consult the MLA will find the MS dated 1960, but the poem was actually written during or shortly after World War II, as its subject suggests. Several copies of *Accent* 7:4 (Winter 1947) contain the last twelve lines of this poem beneath a pasted-down sheet (p. 112) on which lines 19–23 of "Chiffon Velours" are printed. The editors of *Accent* apparently received this poem as early as 1946, had it typeset and printed, and then decided, for what-

ever reason, not to run it. I am grateful to Marisa Januzzi for this observation, which I have independently confirmed by examining two copies of *Accent* containing the paste-down.

43. TIME-BOMB, ca. 1945. First published in *Between Worlds* 1:2 (Spring/Summer 1961, p. 200). This text follows the *BW* version, which is identical to a signed typescript labeled "Selection to: 'Between Worlds' Oct. 1960" (YCAL). *Editor's Note:* It is possible that Gilbert Neiman influenced the extra spaces between words and punctuation in this poem, for upon receiving the first batch of submissions from ML he wrote: "For my part . . . you are not allowing yourself the ample spaces you once did" (GN). But these were not the allowances he was referring to.

44. OMEN OF VICTORY. Composition date unknown, although it can be conjecturally dated ca. 1945, coinciding with the victory of the Allied forces in World War II. This text follows the MS at YCAL. First published in *LBT*. No prior periodical appearance.
Editor's Note: In his foreword to *LBT*, WCW writes: "Mina Loy was endowed from birth with a first rate intelligence facing a shoddy world. When she puts a word down on paper it is clean; that forces her fellows to shy away from it because they are not clean and will be contaminated by her cleanliness. Therefore she has not been a successful writer and couldn't care less. But it has hurt her chances of being known. . . . The essence of her style is its directness in which she is exceeded by no one." WCW ends his foreword by quoting "Omen of Victory" in full, describing it as "an epigrammatic gem which many of the poets of our own day might follow for its punch and delicate if sardonic humor."

45. FILM-FACE. Composition date unknown, although presumably written sometime after Marie Dressler's death in 1934. This poem has not appeared in any periodical or collection, although it was printed in a limited-edition broadside in 1995. The present text is identical to a signed typescript at MLA, whereon ML noted that it was submitted to *Between Worlds* in 1960.
Editor's Note: Actress Marie Dressler (Leila Marie Koerber [1869–1934]) made her screen debut in *Tillie's Punctured Romance* (1914), in which she co-starred with Charlie Chaplin. A homely woman of considerable girth, she was America's biggest box-office draw in the early 1930s. She won an Oscar for her lead role in *Min and Bill* (1930), a romantic comedy about a scruffy waterfront couple. In an earlier stage production, Mina and Bill (WCW) played husband and wife in Alfred Kreymborg's *Lima Beans* (1916) at the Provincetown Playhouse, a poetic playlet in which romance is punctured by vegetables. Marie Dressler and Myrna Loy were both MGM actresses in the 1930s and worked with some of the same directors. Only coincidence connects these alluring facts.

46. FAUN FARE, 1948. First published in *Between Worlds* 2:1 (Fall/Winter 1962, pp. 28-30). A typescript dated December 27, 1948, is preserved at YCAL. The present text follows the *BW* version, which in turn follows the MS in all substantives. I have made the following emendations to the published text:

19: ocular] acular
24: tongue] tonque
38: addict] addicy

Editor's Note: This poem's publication marked the last magazine publication of ML's work before her death in 1966, and the successful placement of a poem which had earlier been rejected by *New Directions* (GN). Neiman overreaches in his contributor's note; his view is not one that many of his own generation would have shared: "Mina Loy is considered by many to be, despite the paucity of her work, the best poetess in English of the century."

This poem is reminiscent of ML's early satires, but its subject—the sexual ambiguity of male guests at a Manhattan cocktail party—is more surprising, its language more terse, and its perspective, if anything, more unusual. I include this poem with thanks to Jim Powell and in memory of Arthur Cravan (ML's own faun, who had the head of a poet, the body of a boxer).

65: "Evoe" is an exclamatory utterance associated with Bacchanalian orgies, e.g., "wild evoes and howlings" (OED).

47. LETTERS OF THE UNLIVING. Composed June 19, 1949. An edited version of this poem appeared in *LLB82*. No prior periodical appearance. The present text follows the signed and dated typescript at YCAL, with two emendations:

37: calligraphy] caligraphy
78: blasé] blase

Editor's Note: This poem, concerned with time, memory, loss, and the boundaries of identity, is addressed to AC (see n. 18, 19), whom ML once described as "the one other intelligence" she could converse with and whose unexplained disappearance remained one of her life's greatest unassimilables. He is the long-eclipsed author of the "authorless" letters whose "creased leaves," these many years later, still held hostage the poet's irremediably bruised heart. His past words have been preserved, and their pastness opens onto the present in the "calligraphy of recollection." But memory is more punishing than amnesia given "death's erasure/ . . . of the lover."

Well into her seventies, ML was still grieving over her husband's premature "death," describing his body, and speaking of his great "potential." A selection of the letters he had written to her during their brief separation four decades earlier was recently published in Jean-Pierre Begot, ed., *Arthur Cravan: Œuvres (Paris: Editions Ivrea, 1992), pp.155–83. LLB82* contains a superlinear abstraction of AC in the form of ML's diary entries (pp. 317–22), as well as a description of their superlunar bond (xlvii–lxi).

48. HOT CROSS BUM, 1949. First published in *New Directions* 12 (1950, pp. 311–20). A signed and dated (August 30,1949) typescript at YCAL denotes ML's address as 5 Stanton Street. This text is based on the *ND* version, to which I have made several emendations, all following the MS:

   25: delight's] delight"s
  128: hot-cross] hot-cros
  149: crossroads] cross-roads
  167: ragged] rugged
  183: adamic] academic
  213: anomoly] anomaly
  242: ebon aide] ebonaide

The 1949 MS. carries several other variations from the first published version which I have not incorporated into the present text. Some are clearly spelling errors, but others bear reporting, since it is not clear at what stage (or by whom) the changes were made:

    9: to Ecstasia] in Ecstasia
   35: faces] Faces
   50: directions] direction
  177a: {line deleted}] in somehow irresponsive ideals
  221: once patroned] patroned
  222: entice] console

Editor's Note: Kenneth Rexroth, in 1944, ended his essay (n. 17) on ML with a strong exhortation to his publisher at New Directions Press: "Mr. Laughlin, the 'Five Young Poets' are still Eliot, Stevens, Williams, Moore, Loy—get busy." Whether at Rexroth's urging or not, James Laughlin did engage in correspondence with ML; the publication of this poem in *ND* is the one tangible result. Laughlin also considered publishing her novel *Insel*, but eventually explained that he could not do so "due to the heavy backlog we have." He suggested she send it a friend of his at Simon & Schuster, where it was also rejected. The novel was eventually published by Black Sparrow Press in 1991.

"Communal cot" (l. 270) obviously refers to the space of the modern street within the poem's context; it is also the title of one of ML's cloth and cardboard constructions of street scenes exhibited at the Bodley Gallery in 1959 (see pl. 29, *LLB*82), now in the collection of William Copley.

49. AN AGED WOMAN. Composition date unknown, but certainly a late poem. An edited draft version of this poem first appeared posthumously in *LLB*82, under the title "An Old Woman", following the title of an earlier HV (YCAL). No prior periodical appearance. The present text is identical to ML's revised HV at YCAL.

Editor's Note: The HV is unmistakably signed and dated prospectively at the bottom of the page in ML's hand: "Mina Loy. July 12, 1984." I have to assume this postdating is deliberate, given the question ("is the impossible / possible to senility[?])" addressed to the prosopoeia in possession of the old woman's body and the issue raised in the first stanza about the future's (in)exploitability. The "Bulbous stranger" in the mirror, the bloated beldam who has invaded the erstwhile slim and athletic self, is an alien self, an "excessive incognito / . . . only to be exorcised by death." The use of the present perfect tense in the poem's first, third, and final stanzas describes the speaker's knowledge at the time of speaking, but if we take the "future" date of composition into account, this knowledge is still premonitional. At the time of composition, the poem's very existence was called into question by its date, making the spectral encounter between the self and its reflected image theoretical. The mind's incubus was thus as subject to elimination by senility as its body's was by death. An attempt, perhaps, to blur the lines between spatial, temporal, and psychological modalities; and a teleology, if not a demonstration, of dementia's tricky logic.

50. MOREOVER, THE MOON — — — . Composition date unknown. First published in *LLB*82. No prior periodical appearance. This text is based on the MS at YCAL, to which I have made one emendation:

    13: innuendoes] inuendos

V. Excavations & Precisions
(Prose 1914–1925)

51. APHORISMS ON FUTURISM, January 1914. First published in Alfred Stieglitz's epochal quarterly, *Camera Work* 45 (January [June] 1914, pp. 13–15). A single signed, dated HV of this work survives (ASP); it varies from the first published version only in accidentals. In the HV, ampersands replace "and" throughout, and line 9 *EXPLODES* with *LIGHT* with more calligraphic flourish than can be expressed typographically. I have made two emendations to the published version, the first based on standard orthography and the second following the HV. Each paragraph is counted as a line. Thus:

    7: dilapidated] delapidated
    34: ambiente] ambient

Editor's Note: This composition dates from ML's Futurist period and marks her first recorded appearance in print. A printed leaf of the *CW* text at YCAL bears ML's penciled substitution of the word "modern" for "future" and "Modernism" for "Futurism" throughout. ML probably made these notes after abandoning her Futurist allegiance; although she might have retrospectively preferred to call this piece "Aphorisms on Modernism," I have retained the original title.

In form, its debt to Futurism is clear; its content also reflects Marinetti's influence. Among publications by Futurist-inspired women, "Aphorisms on Futurism" was preceded only by the writings of parodist Flora Bonheur (*Diary of a Futurist Woman*, 1914) and manifesto writer Valentine de Saint-Point (see n. 52).

52. FEMINIST MANIFESTO. November 1914. First published (inaccurately) in *LLB*82. For this edition, I have followed ML's signed and dated HV (MDLP), with the exception of the emendations noted below. Since the manifesto was written as prose, I have not preserved the lineation of the HV, except where a pronounced break signals a new paragraph or transition.

  3: psychological] pschycological
  4: centuries] centuaries
  21: are] is
  46: character] charactar
  56: ridiculously] rediculously
  68: psychic] pschycic
  80: desire] disire

Editor's Note: The only known copy of this text was sent to MDL in 1914. The text was still in a provisional state, uncorrected and unfinished, as indicated by ML's apostil to MDL on the first page of the MS: "This is a rough draught beginning of an absolute resubstantiation of the feminist question   give me your opinion—of course it's easily to be proved fallacious—There is no truth ——anywhere." In a subsequent letter to MDL, ML wrote: "By the way— that fragment of Feminist tirade I sent you—flat? I find the destruction of virginity—*so* daring don't you think—had been suggested by some other woman years ago—see Havelock Ellis—I feel rather hopeless of devotion to the Woman-cause—Slaves will believe that chains are protectors . . . they are the more efficient for the coward—." Later in the same letter, ML refers to Frances Simpson Stevens (1894–1976), the American Futurist painter who had rented ML's studio at 54, Costa San Giorgio, Florence, in 1913. "My dear, I hear that you see Frances Stevens in New York. What do you think of her? I have got the impression from her letter that America is the home of middle class hypocrisy. Is it, outside the charmed circle you preside? Do tell me" (MDLP). When she referred disapprovingly to Stevens's "virginal hysterics" over Margaret Sanger's "idiotic book of preventive propaganda," ML knew that she was directing her comments to interested ears. MDL had arranged Stevens's introduction to ML, and was the *grande dame* of Manhattan's most important avant-garde salon, where Sanger, Ellis, and many other sexual reformers were guests.

This manifesto was probably written in part in negation to FTM's "The Founding and Manifesto of Futurism" (1909). It may also have been conceived to counterbalance feminist *manqué* and French poet Valentine de Saint-Point's [pseud. of Desglans de Cessiat-Vercell, 1875–1953] "Manifesto of the Futurist Woman" (1912) and "Futurist Manifesto of Lust" (1913). Saint-Point's manifestos announced the birth of a strong and instinctive superwoman and affirmed the rights of female sexual desire. Loy's conception of a superior female race is further developed in "Psycho-Democracy," where she diagrams a vision of "compound existence" between advanced human beings of both sexes.

Rachel Blau DuPlessis has written convincingly of this work's problematic relationship to the feminine ideology of "Love Songs" in Ralph Cohen, ed., *Studies in Historical Change* (Charlottesville: University Press of Virginia, 1992, pp. 264–91). The notes to her essay " 'Seismic Orgasm': Sexual Intercourse, Gender Narratives, and Lyric Ideology in Mina Loy" point out regrettable editorial errors and mistranscriptions introduced in the *LLB82* rendering of this text, which I have tried to correct in the present edition.

53. MODERN POETRY. Composition date unknown, ca. 1925. First published in *Charm* 3:3 (April 1925, pp. 16–17, 71). NOMS. The present edition follows verbatim the first and only published version.

Editor's Note: This text represents ML's only known critical discussion of modern poetry. As such, it offers a valuable insight into her views of her contemporaries, and an original, personal, and mature glimpse of her taste in contemporary poetry. Along with her essays on GS and Joseph Cornell, it is one of the very few examples we have of ML's attempt to establish a critical voice. It is also the only published text that I know of in which she discusses her own diction and what it means to write in the American-immigrant idiom. I discovered this text well after the publication of *LLB82*, which raises the possibility of other unknown Loy publications being found in similarly obscure or non-literary periodicals. *Charm* was an eclectic magazine published in the 1920s, devoted to women's fashion and clothing. Djuna Barnes contributed several articles to it, some under the pseudonym Lady Lydia Steptoe. Given that its content was for the most part of a non-literary nature, it is not surprising that its existence was not recorded in Hoffman, Allen, and Ulrich, eds., *The Little Magazine* (Princeton University Press, 1947). Copies of *Charm* are extremely rare. The New York Public Library has a run; I am interested in learning of copies catalogued elsewhere.

54. PRECEPTORS OF CHILDHOOD, OR THE NURSES OF MARAQUITA. Composition date unknown, ca. 1922. First published in *Playboy: A Portfolio of Art and Satire* 2:1 (first quarter, 1923, p. 12). Signed, undated MS at YCAL. I have made one emendation to the published version:

III.4: tassel] tassle

Editor's Note: The original *Playboy*, edited by Egmont Arens, was a quarterly review devoted to "informal, spontaneous, uncensored and frankly experimental material by "those who are trying to blaze new paths of artistic expression . . . against the dullness, ugliness and backwardlookingness of our own day." *Playboy* had earlier published a reproduction of a watercolor by ML in its May 1921 issue (p. 22). This autobiographical sketch has remained uncollected until now. In it, ML recalls her own childhood governesses by their actual names, but fictionalizes herself as Maraquita. I thank Marisa Januzzi for bringing this text to my attention.

55. AUTO-FACIAL-CONSTRUCTION. Composition date unknown. NOMS. First published as a promotional pamphlet for private distribution (Florence: Tipografia Giuntina, 1919). The present text is a verbatim transcription of the first published text.

Editor's Note: The 1919 brochure was signed "Mina Loy, Sociétaire du Salon d'Automne, Paris," raising the possibility that this bizarre scheme may have been conceived as early as 1906, when ML was elected a member of the Salon d'Automne. More likely, she was trading on an earlier credential and conceived the idea of offering her services as a prosopologist following her return to Italy after the disappearance of AC, when she was desperate for income. This was the first of many entrepreneurial attempts ML made to pitch business ideas to clients. In a letter to MDL (n.d., 1920?) she wrote: "Am enclosing a prospectus of a new method I shall teach when not drawing or writing about art. It came as a most unexpected revelation. And it works. I think the life-force inspired me with it to solve the problem of keeping bodies alive without prostituting art." In a later letter to MDL, ML lamented, "I have been too ill to make my facial discovery convincing" (MDLP).

GP may have influenced ML's thinking about facial destiny; as the self-described ugliest man in Italy, he was preoccupied with the effect of his appearance on the formation of his character, and was given to speculating on the relationship between visage and destiny.

I include this text not for its literary value but because it represents an important aspect of ML's creative imagination not evident in her other writings. Throughout her life ML was preoccupied with income-producing schemes and brought to bear her considerable esoteric knowledge of art, technology, and human nature to advance practical experiments, test entrepreneurial ideas, and promote business strategies in order to pay the rent and support her children. This text documents one of her many ideas which failed, but she was indefatigable in her attempts to file the next patent or launch another business that might succeed. Her design and manufacture of lamps and lampshades in Paris in the 1920s attained a certain amount of commercial success and earned her notice in the design world of her own time as well as a place in the subsequent history of industrial design (e.g., Mel Byars, *The Design Encyclopedia* [London: Laurence King, 1994], pp. 340–41). Surprisingly, not a single example of her work as a *lampiste* is known to survive. I am still in search of examples.

Three Early Poems

These three poems are published here for the first time. They were composed in 1914; signed and dated HVs of all three poems are preserved in MDLP. ML wrote them in Florence and sent them to MDL in New York, hoping that she would get them published in *The Masses*, whose editors and finances MDL backed. In terms of composition they barely predate ML's so-called Futurist poems, but in normative terms they clearly belong to a less mature stage of authorship. We know from her autobiographical writings that ML produced poems before 1914, but these are apparently the earliest examples to have survived. Given the archival situation, it is unlikely that any earlier poems will surface.

Although these "first fruits" are clearly the work of apprenticeship, I include them here because they reveal certain tendencies in ML's work that were soon to ripen and establish a baseline from which to measure her later achievement. As control texts, they provide a perspective on the development of her later work which has not been available before. I have followed ML's lineation in my transcriptions, although "The Prototype" is closer to prose than verse; a prose diagram of an incipient poem, it verges toward verse only in its final lines. Notes on specific poems follow:

I have made no emendations to the HV of "The Beneficent Garland," signed and dated January 1914 (therefore ML's earliest known poem).

I have made two emendations to the HV of "The Prototype," signed February 28, 1914:

9: tinsel] tinsil

36: inebriating] enebriating

The text of "Involutions" is reproduced here with no emendations to the 1914 HV.

The Beneficent Garland

To hang about the knees of the gods,
The first-fruits of the awful odds
'Gainst which man till'd the soil.

What are then these first fruits, I pray
Swelling at night, to ripen by day
Such sorrows of their toil?

Fruits of this mystery are they born
The baby & the ear of corn,
Hunger & drawing breath

The laboured seasons of the year
The rise & fall of love & fear
All leaping into death.

See the angel carrying the swag
Of blossoms culled with sweat & fag
He is man's guardian.

But what use have the gods for such flowers
Of earth, up in their sheeny bowers
On Heaven's meridian?

Their smell is the joy of His nostril
Breathing the essence of the Gospel
Out in a narrow flame

For the gods supporting the million
Miles of darkness round His pavilion
Are lighted by that same.

The Prototype

In the Duomo, on Xmas Eve, midnight
a cold wax baby is born— born of the
light of 1,000 candles.
He is quite perfect, of that perfection
which means immunity from
the inconsistencies of Life.

Perfect in pink-&-whiteness, in blue-
eyedness, in yellow-silk-curledness
& nearly as bright as the tinsel star
that rises on his forehead.

Worship him, for his infinitesimal
mouth has no expansiveness for a puck-
ering to the heart-saving wail of the
new-born Hungry One.

In the Duomo at Xmas Eve, midnight,
there is another baby, a horrible little
baby—made of half warm flesh;
flesh that is covered with sores—carried
by a half-broken mother.

And I who am called heretic,
and the only follower in Christ's foot-steps
among this crowd adoring a wax doll
—for I alone am worshipping the poor
sore baby—the child of sex igno-
rance & poverty.

I am on my knees humbly before
him, praying, not to a god, but to
humanity's social consciousness, to
do for that mother & that child in the light, what
the priests have tried to do in the dark.

For that half-broken mother the child
on the high altar is the prototype,
the prototype of all babies as they
might have been.

She has this unique Xmas present from
the church, an inebriating glimpse of
something that a baby is supposed to look
like; she is shown the Perfection of which
the offspring & object of all her love is
             the battered symbol.

Blow out the candles—
Throw away the wax-baby
Use the churches as night-shelters
Come into the Daylight & preach
             a New Gospel

       Let them eat—
O let them love—
And let their babies be
             pink & white.

Involutions

When the last flower blows in the first seed
Carried away by the thought of a wind
When the first concept fills the last deed
Shews us the longest way we have sinned

The last step is the mountain's measure
Trod deep in the long flat face of Fraud
And the pain's gasp, the length of pleasure
In the Saint's wounds—the soul of a Bawd.

With the last chains, forge the first freedom
Renunciation's claim on the lover
The last King of a crucified kingdom
Destroying himself to find his brother.

"Love Songs" (1923)

In 1923, ML's first book was published by Robert McAlmon's Contact Publishing Co. (Paris), which that same year had published Ernest Hemingway's *Three Stories and Ten Poems*. *Lunar Baedecker* [*sic*] was announced for $1.50. (It was recently listed—and sold—for $1,500.) A modest paperback, it was printed on what even then was considered cheap paper, in an edition of several hundred copies, of which at least one copy was bound in green boards with silver endpapers. It contained fewer than twenty poems, if we count the suite of thirteen "Love Songs" as a single poem. In *LB*, the individually numbered sections of "Love Songs" were not only presented in a different order than the original thirty-four; many sections were eliminated altogether, while several entirely new lines appeared. "Love Songs" was an excavated skeleton of the former body, absent some bones.

Perhaps because it is shorter and more accessible, the 1923 "Love Songs" has been much more frequently anthologized than the 1917 "Songs to Joannes." Jonathan Williams considered the *LB* version the "text of record" when he published *LBT*, but this was his decision, not ML's. Any serious consideration of "Love Songs" should begin with the *Others* publication of "Songs to Joannes," which is printed in the main text of this edition. For comparative purposes the 1923 renovation should then be taken into account. Likewise, readers interested in a detailed textual and critical history of this poem should refer to n. 15 (Appendix B).

The 1923 "Love Songs" lacks the body heat of the 1917 "Songs to Joannes." The later version tends to be suggestive and abstract, where the early version is more explicit and graphic. Comparing the foundation text and the instaurational text offers a rare opportunity for critical speculation about how and why ML revised her poems. Did the scandal over the erotic content of the 1915 (*Others*) publication of "Love Songs" or ML's awareness of the censorship problems facing James Joyce's *Ulysses* (n. 26) prompt her to censor her own work? Would the publication by an expatriate press raise the eyebrows of customs officials when the publication was checked for clearance in the United States? Might this explain the elimination of some of the earlier version's sexually explicit passages? In 1982, I speculated as much; apparently part of the U.S. shipment was impounded. In a (July 16, 1930) letter addressed to her older daughter, ML suggested that she favored obscure language not only for its own sake, but to "get by the censor!"

The *LB* text of "Love Songs" is printed verbatim below, with the exception of two emendations:

VII. 11: sarsenet] sarsanet

X.6: archetypal] architypal

Love Songs (1923)

I

Spawn of fantasies
Sifting the appraisable
Pig Cupid   his rosy snout
Rooting erotic garbage
"Once upon a time"
Pulls a weed   white star-topped
Among wild oats sown in mucous membrane
I would   an eye in a Bengal light
Eternity in a sky-rocket
Constellations in an ocean
Whose rivers run no fresher
Than a trickle of saliva

These are suspect places

I must live in my lantern
Trimming subliminal flicker
Virginal   to the bellows
Of experience
                    Colored glass.

II

At your mercy
Our Universe
Is only
A colorless onion
You derobe
Sheath by sheath
          Remaining

A disheartening odour
About your nervy hands

III

     Night
Heavy with shut-flower's nightmares
— — — — — — — — — — —
     Noon
Curled to the solitaire
Core of the
Sun

IV

Evolution fall foul of
Sexual equality
Prettily miscalculate
Similitude

Unnatural selection
Breed such sons and daughters
As shall jibber at each other
Uninterpretable cryptonyms
Under the moon

Give them some way of braying brassily
For caressive calling
Or to homophonous hiccoughs
Transpose the laugh
Let them suppose that tears
Are snowdrops or molasses
Or anything
Than human insufficiencies
Begging dorsal vertebrae

Let meeting be the turning

To the antipodean
And Form   a blurr
Anything
Than seduce them
To the one
As simple satisfaction
For the other

V

Shuttle-cock and battle-door
A little pink-love
And feathers are strewn

VI

Let Joy go solace-winged
To flutter whom she may concern

VII

Once in a mezzanino
The starry ceiling
Vaulted an unimaginable family
Bird-like abortions
With human throats
And Wisdom's eyes
Who wore lamp-shade red dresses
And woolen hair

One bore a baby
In a padded porte-enfant
Tied with a sarsenet ribbon
To her goose's wings

But for the abominable shadows
I would have lived

Among their fearful furniture
To teach them to tell me their secrets
Before I guessed
— Sweeping the brood clean out

VIII

Midnight empties the street
— — — To the left a boy
—One wing has been washed in rain
The other will never be clean any more —
Pulling door-bells to remind
Those that are snug
        To the right a haloed ascetic
        Threading houses
Probes wounds for souls
— The poor can't wash in hot water —
And I don't know which turning to take —

IX

We might have coupled
In the bed-ridden monopoly of a moment
Or broken flesh with one another
At the profane communion table
Where wine is spill't on promiscuous lips

We might have given birth to a butterfly
With the daily-news
Printed in blood on its wings

X

In some
Prenatal plagiarism
Fœtal buffoons
Caught tricks

— — — — —
From archetypal pantomime
Stringing emotions
Looped aloft
— — — —

For the blind eyes
That Nature knows us with
And the most of Nature   is green
— — — — — — — — — — —

XI

Green things grow
Salads
For the cerebral
Forager's revival . . .
And flowered flummery
Upon bossed bellies
Of mountains
Rolling in the sun

XII

Shedding our petty pruderies
From slit eyes

We sidle up
To Nature
— — — that irate pornographist

XIII

The wind stuffs the scum of the white street
Into my lungs and my nostrils
Exhilarated birds
Prolonging flight into the night
Never reaching — — — — — — —

Other Writings

This list records alphabetically by title the first published appearance of all of Mina Loy's known published works which are not included in the present edition. I am not reporting second or later appearances in magazines or anthologies, nor am I distinguishing posthumous works from those published during her lifetime. This distinction can be easily made by the reader; ML died in 1966. The notes on individual texts in Appendix B contain information on the first published appearance of all works included in the main text of this volume.

Poetry

"America*A Miracle." LLB82, pp. 227–31.

"Anglo-Mongrels and the Rose." *The Little Review* 9:3 (Spring 1923), pp. 10–18; 9:4 (Autumn/Winter 1923), pp. 41–51; *Contact Collection of Contemporary Writers* (Paris: Three Mountains Press, 1925), pp. 137–94.

"Aviator's Eyes." Larry Krantz, "Three Neglected Poets," *Wagner Literary Magazine* [formerly *Nimbus*] (Spring 1959), p. 54.

"Birth of Melody." LLB82, 241.

"Brain." LLB82, p. 257.

"Breath Bank." LLB82, p. 254.

"Brilliant Confusion of Brilliance." LLB82, p. 234.

"Ceiling at Dawn." LLB82, p. 242.

"Child Chanting." LLB82, p. 239.

"Continuity." LLB82, p. 255.

"Desert of the Ganges." LLB82, p. 252.

"Echo." LLB82, p. 240.

"Evolution". LLB82, p. 256.

"Hilarious Israel." *Accent* 7:2 (Winter 1947), pp. 110–11.

"I Almost Saw God in the Metro." LLB82, p. 248.

"Impossible Opus." *Between Worlds* 1:2 (Spring/Summer 1961), pp. 199–200.

"L'Inavouable Enfant." LLB82, p. 236.

"Maiden Song." LLB82, p. 237.

"The Mediterranean Sea." LLB82, pp. 250–51.

"Mother Earth." LLB82, p. 253.

"Negro Dancer." *Between Worlds* 1:2 (Spring/Summer 1961), p. 202.

"Overnight." LLB82, p. 258.

"Portrait of a Nun." LLB82, p. 260.

"Repassed Platform." LLB82, p. 249.

"Revelation." LBT, pp. 73–74.

"The Song of the Nightingale Is Like the Scent of Syringa." LBT, p. 80.

"Songge Byrd." LLB82, p. 238.

"Stravinski's Flute." LBT, p. 77.

"Surfeit of Controversy." LLB82, p. 232.

"There Is No Love Alone." LLB82, p. 233.

"To You." *Others* 3:1 (July 1916), pp. 27–28.

"Transformation Scene." LBT, pp. 78–79.

"Untitled." *Between Worlds* 2:1 (Fall/Winter 1962), p. 27. YCAL MS title is "In Extremis." Published as "Show Me a Saint Who Suffered" [first line of poem] in LLB82.

"Vision on Broadway." LLB82, p. 247.

"White Petunia." LLB82, p. 243.

Prose

"Colossus" (memoir). Roger L. Conover, "Mina Loy's Colossus: Arthur Cravan Undressed," in *Dada/Surrealism* 14 (1985); reprinted in Rudolf E. Kuenzli, ed., *New York Dada* (New York: Willis Locker & Owens, 1986), pp. 102–19.

"Gertrude Stein" (essay). *transatlantic review* 2:3 (October 1924), pp. 305–9; and *transatlantic review* 2:4 (November 1924), pp. 427–30.

"In . . . Formation" (polemic). *Blind Man* 1 (April 10, 1917), p. 7.

Insel (novel). Elizabeth Arnold, ed., with foreword by Roger L. Conover (Santa Rosa: Black Sparrow Press, 1991).

"John Rodker's Frog" (response). *The Little Review* 7:3 (September–December 1920), pp. 56–57.

"Notes on Religion" (essay fragments). Edited and introduced by Keith Tuma, *Sulfur* 27 (Fall 1990), pp. 13–16.

"O Marcel—otherwise I Also Have Been to Louise's" (vignette). *The Blind Man* 2 (May 1917), pp. 11–12. Reprinted in *View* 5:1 (March 1945), p. 35, as "O Marcel: or I Too Have Been to Louise's," with an autobiographical note by ML.

"The Pamperers" (drama). *The Dial* 69:1 (July 1920), pp. 65–88.

"Pas de Commentaires! Louis M. Eilshemius" (profile). *The Blind Man* 2 (May 1917), pp. 11–12.

"Phenomenon in American Art" (review). LLB82, pp. 300–2.

Psycho-Democracy (pamphlet). Florence: Tipografia Peri & Rossi, 1920. Reprinted in *The Little Review* 12 (Autumn 1921), pp. 14–19.

"Questionnaire" (interview). *The Little Review* 12:2 (May 1929), p. 46.

"Street Sister" (fiction). Bronte Adams and Trudi Tate, eds., *That Kind of Woman* (London: Virago Press, 1991), pp. 41–42.

"Summer Night in a Florentine Slum" (vignette). *Contact* 1 (December 1920), pp. 6–7.

"Towards the Unknown" (questionnaire). *View* 1 (February/March 1942), p. 10.

Two Plays ["Collision" and "Cittabapini"] (drama). *Rogue* 1:6 (June 15, 1915), pp. 15–16.

Tables of Contents

LUNAR BAEDEKER
(Paris: Contact Publishing Co., 1923)

· LUNAR BAEDEKER AND TIME-TABLES
(Highlands, N.C.: Jonathan Williams Publisher [Jargon 23], 1958)

*From "Anglo-Mongrels and the Rose."

Love Songs (I–XIII)
Three Italian Pictures
    I. The Costa San Giorgio
    II. July in Vallombrosa
    III. Costa Magic
Parturition

II.* *Poems from* CONTACT COLLECTION OF CONTEMPORARY WRITERS
(1925)
    The Anglo-Mystics of the Rose
    Enter Esau
    Ova Begins to take Notice
    Ova has Governesses
    Christ's Regrettable Reticence
    Religious Instruction

III. Later Poems
    Revelation
    Omen of Victory
    On Third Avenue: Part 2
    Stravinski's Flute
    Transformation Scene
    The Song of the Nightingale is Like the Scent of Syringa
    Jules Pascin

*Selections from "Anglo-Mongrels and the Rose" in *Contact Collection of Contemporary Writers* (Paris: Three Mountains Press, 1925).

Acknowledgments

This work is indebted to all Loy scholarship, past and present. My gain from studying Loy criticism has been immense, and I hope that debt will continue to deepen as Loy scholarship develops and matures. There are several scholars whose contributions have been particularly important. I first want to acknowledge the importance of Marisa Januzzi's work to my own. In many respects, this edition is the result of a collaboration unlike any I have known. Had Marisa not been so generous in sharing her research with me, and so able in arguing points with me, this work would lack much of the integrity I hope it has. The work of Carolyn Burke, Loy's biographer and steadfast critic, has also mattered to me for many years. I began my work on Loy twenty years ago, at about the same time that Carolyn began hers. She not only understands, but shares my dedication to this poet. I feel a unique bond with her. From my work with both these scholars, community has grown.

I thank the many graduate students who have written to me about their research on Loy, and the many professors who are now assigning Loy in their classes. They are now too many to mention, but this book was prepared largely with them in mind. Kenneth Fields and Virginia Kouidis wrote their dissertations on Loy at a time when it was even more courageous to do so than it is now. Kouidis's monograph on Mina Loy was the first book published on the poet and remains a useful introduction to the life and work. I have learned from Rachel Blau DuPlessis's criticism on Loy. More recently, Marjorie Perloff has been writing about Loy; her attention is not only noticed but needed.

No words can express the value I place on my friendships with Mina Loy's daughters, Joella Bayer and Fabienne Benedict, nor could my work on Loy have begun or continued in as satisfying a way without them. I miss their husbands, Herbert Bayer and Fritz Benedict, who were always present during our early meetings and who had wonderful stories to relate about "Mama Mina."

In the late 1970s I approached Jonathan Williams with a proposal for putting together a centennial edition of Mina Loy's poems, aware that, twenty years earlier, he was the only publisher in America astute or brave enough to bring out a book of her poems. She was still alive at the time and encouraged him not to be depressed when the book didn't get the attention he thought it deserved. Without those editions, this one would not exist. Jonathan deserves a medal for his support of lost voices and poetic causes. I hope he sees the publication of this book as a validation of his efforts.

I would like to thank my editors at Farrar Straus Giroux—Jonathan Galassi, Paul Elie, and Lynn Warshow. I have been in the editing business a long time, but I have learned something new from each of them.

Poet Thom Gunn is perhaps Mina Loy's most able reader. I realized this only when we gave a reading together in New York last year. I thank him for his generous suggestions and corrections, and for his own poetry. Jim Powell I have never met, but he is also among the poets, after Kenneth Rexroth and Gunn, who have most consistently advocated for Mina Loy, and among the critics whose readings and e-mail messages I have most benefited from. Jerome Rothenberg and Eliot Weinberger are two others whose support of Loy has made a difference.

Francis Naumann and Terry Keller know how much they have done to help me in the fine-tuning of this edition. I am extremely grateful to both of them, Terry for her unparalleled vocabulary and Francis for his archive and memory. Michael Barson provided me with answers to several nocturnal questions I could have addressed to no one else. Cita Scott, Martica Sawin, Thomas Redshaw, Joseph Rykwert, Robert Bertholf, and Steven Watson did the same. My interest in and knowlege of poetry owes much to Harry George, who elects to remain an unknown poet but who I hope will one day choose to publish his work, or to produce an edition of the work of Louis Coxe, who taught him. Laurence Cohen solved a number of editorial riddles for me, and Thomas Clayton provided some. I thank them both. Keith Tuma supplied a comment that was most important when I was almost ready to give up on the notes. I have also profited from his writing on Loy. Lisa Jacobs made some unexpected discoveries pertaining to Mina Loy along the way.

Virginia Conover, John Unterecker, and Donald Hendrie, Jr., are now gone, but will always be in the background of anything I write, as will my sister and brothers, and father, all of whom I treasure. It helped, when I wondered who would be listening, to imagine certain friends reading this book: Sabina Engel, Serge Fauchereau, Kurt Forster, Lyman Gilmore, George Hersey, John Irving, Damon Krukowski, Alberto Perez-Gomez, Irma Romero, Cristina Sanmartin. It also helped to know that other friends would still be there whether I ever finished editing or not, like Kenn Guimond, Jim Sterling, Jack Montgomery, and Krzysztof Wodiczko.

Suzanne Tise knows her contribution.

Without the cooperation of Patricia Willis, curator of the Yale Collection of American Literature at Yale's Beinecke Library, and her predecessor, Donald Gallup, neither this edition nor my many visits to that fabulous resource would have been as rich.

Now for the magic part. My two sons, Case and Strand, are the deep poetry of my life, and have forgiven me more weekend ski passes and morning soccer practices than I would like to acknowledge in order to complete this book. I hope they know I would rather have been with them. The other magic part: Anna Ginn has been this book's longest and closest companion. She knows everything about the other woman—Mina Loy—who shares our house, and has participated in the intimate details of this project more than anyone else. She has also been a better editor, critic, fact checker, and proofreader than any I have ever paid. And in much larger ways than these, she has made the completion of this book possible. The simplest words are saved for last, and said with the most love: Thank you, Anna. Thank you, boys.

R.L.C.